THE MESSAGE OF
THE NEW TESTAMENT

The Message
of the
New Testament

BY

ARCHIBALD M. HUNTER

B.D., Ph.D., D.Phil.

YATES PROFESSOR OF NEW TESTAMENT GREEK AND EXEGESIS
MANSFIELD COLLEGE, OXFORD

PHILADELPHIA

THE WESTMINSTER PRESS

Published in Great Britain
as
The Unity of the New Testament

PRINTED IN THE UNITED STATES OF AMERICA

CONTENTS

CHAPTER ONE

THE QUEST FOR UNITY

Dr. JOHN BROWN, that "beloved physician" and no less beloved man of letters, in a tribute to his father relates how a great change in his life affected his studies and preaching: "He then left the ordinary commentators and men who write about meanings and flutter round the circumference and corners; he was bent on the centre, on seeing with his own eyes, on touching with his own fingers, the pearl of great price." [1]

These words are a parable of what is happening in the world of New Testament scholarship to-day. Anyone conversant with the most recent work on the New Testament must have sensed in it a change of approach, a change of direction. The scholars are leaving " the circumference and the corners ": they are " bent on the centre." Hitherto their method has been largely centrifugal; now it is becoming more and more centripetal. There is a growing recognition of the essential unity of the New Testament and of the need for synthesis. That there was some such inherent unity, a unity that transcended and dominated all diversities, we must suppose to have been the conviction of the men who helped to form the canon of the New Testament. That there is such a unity and that recent New Testament study is making it ever plainer, it is the purpose of these pages to show.

"The New Testament," says A. H. MacNeile, in his *Introduction*,[2] "is a collection of masterpieces of spiritual music." Yet if there are many musicians (and there are

9

at least a dozen) playing different instruments, one dominant theme sounds through all their music.

What is that dominant theme? And how shall we describe it?

Some years ago a distinguished Oxford scholar [3] desiring an answer to this question sought out several New Testament experts and put to them this query: " If you had to express the unity of the New Testament in one word or phrase, what would it be? " To be sure, it was rather a staggering question. Not surprisingly, therefore, the first man accosted, a man whose fame as a researcher into Gospel origins was world-wide, replied by asking for notice of the question. But the others, less hesitant, gave their answers. One said, " The Holy Spirit "; another, " The Fatherhood of God "; another, " Sonship "; and the last, " Redemption." No doubt if the questionnaire had been pursued farther, more interesting answers would have emerged. Dr. L. P. Jacks, if he had been asked, would apparently have answered " Immortality." [4] And so on.

Quot doctores, tot sententiæ. The diversity of these answers shows how radically the experts differ on this fundamental question. But can we really rest content with any of these answers? Each fastens on something which, while it is an important element in New Testament Christianity, is after all only one element. None of the answers is sufficiently inclusive. To find the unifying element in " the Holy Spirit " is tantamount to identifying the new hope and gladness kindled in our hearts when Nature wakes from her winter sleep, with the Spring itself. To sum it up in " the Fatherhood of God " is like telling a man what *Hamlet* is about and forgetting to mention the Prince of Denmark. " Sonship " no doubt stands for something very precious in New Testament Christianity; but, apart from the fact that " John " never calls believers " sons," the word will simply not do as a unifying formula. A certain wit once suggested that we ought to arrange the various heresies of the Church in order of merit: if that principle were applied in the present problem, many would no doubt put the last answer first. But the term " redemption " is too circumscribed in its connotation. We need something more comprehensive, something that will do better justice to "the manifold wisdom of God " as it meets us in the pages of the New Testament.

Can we find such a term?

There is no point in going abroad for a word if we have one equally good at home; but in the present case the Germans have a single word which answers the purpose, and we have not.[5] That word is *Heilsgeschichte*, a word with New Testament warrant behind it (see Acts xiii. 26; cf. Eph. i. 13). The dominant theme of the New Testament is " the story of salvation "; the word " salvation " being used here in its widest sense.[6]

This *Heilsgeschichte* of which the New Testament speaks from beginning to end, includes many things — all indeed that is suggested by the answers already quoted — but chiefly three things; and these (to use the technical terms) are: Christology, Ecclesiology, and Soteriology. In other words, the *Heilsgeschichte* treats of a Saviour, a Saved (and saving) People, and the means of Salvation. And these three are at bottom one — three strands in a single cord, a trinity in unity. For the " story " is of the consummation of God's saving purpose for his People (Ecclesiology) through the sending of his Messiah (Christology) and of the means of Salvation (Soteriology).

" The consummation of God's saving purpose for his People . . ." we said. Thus to define the central theme of the New Testament is to see it in its proper Biblical perspective — to see it as the apostolic writers always see it, to see it as Jesus himself saw it (witness the parable of the Wicked Husbandman (Mark xii. 1 f.), which is the *Heilsgeschichte* in brief), namely, against the background of the Old Testament. In short, it is to see the New Testament as the fulfilment of the Old and to take seriously our Lord's own words: "Think not that I came to destroy the Law and the Prophets: I came not to destroy but to fulfil" (Matt. v. 17). Seen thus, the Bible is not only a collection of records describing the development of religious ideas among Israelites, Jews, and Christians, but also and chiefly the story of God's saving purpose for his People begun with the deliverance from Egypt, continued in his later dealings with them recorded in Old Testament history and prophecy, and consummated in the sending of his Son the Messiah:

> God, who to glean the vineyard of His choosing,
>   Sent them evangelists till day was done,
> Bore with the churls, their wrath and their refusing,
>   Gave at the last the glory of His Son.[7]

For, *pace* Marcion and all his successors who would like a religion of *one* Testament, it is the same God who speaks in both the Old and the New Testaments: "God, having of old time spoken unto the fathers in the prophets by divers portions and in divers manners, hath at the end of these days spoken unto us in his Son" (Heb. i. 1–2).

It will be the aim of the following pages to approach the New Testament from the position just outlined and so to reveal its unity. But before we proceed to an exposition of our theme, something must be said concerning another method of study which has been fraught with evil as well as good.

NOTES

1 Letter to John Cairns, D.D.

2 P. 471.

3 Dr. Wheeler Robinson.

4 See *The Confession of an Octogenarian*.

5 On the other hand, we sometimes have a word which the Germans lack. Deissmann confesses how much he envies us the word " gospel " as a native-born equivalent of the Greek *euangelion*.

6 Cf. the use of the word in Anderson Scott's *Christianity according to St. Paul*.

7 Myers, *St. Paul*.

CHAPTER TWO

THE DANGERS OF ANALYSIS

As we are going to speak of unity, let us begin with its opposite. Since the dawn of criticism the approach to the New Testament has been largely analytical. In consequence, the diversity of the New Testament documents has been so emphasized as to become almost axiomatic; and the quest on which we are now started may well appear a quest for the non-existent. Consider what a literary "all sorts" these New Testament scriptures are! Twenty-seven documents in all, written over a period of not less than two generations by at least a dozen hands, and how diverse! First, four documents called "gospels" which defy classification in any conventional literary category: biography in the ancient or modern sense they are not; then a volume of history; then twenty-one documents which we comprehensively label "Epistles," though that term covers many literary types, from a massive theological treatise (Romans) to a private letter (Philemon) and includes a rhetorical homily (Hebrews) and an ethical scrap-book (James); the whole being rounded off with a collection of apocalyptic visions (Revelation).

But it is when we leave *form* to consider *content* that the diversity of the New Testament documents is most striking. The dominant theme of the Synoptic Gospels seems to be "the Kingdom of God"; of the Fourth Gospel, "eternal life"; of St. Paul, being "in Christ"; of Hebrews, "the Priesthood of Christ"; and so on. Eschatology, mysticism, and ethics are interwoven in our documents. If one writer uses the Jewish conception of two Ages, another deals in the Platonic conception of two worlds. If for St. Paul revelation comes through redemption, for St. John the opposite seems true — redemption through revelation; if for St. Paul the essence of soteriology is " justification by faith," St. James insists that " faith without works is dead." If for St. Paul the Law is generally the moral law, for the writer to the Hebrews it is generally the ceremonial law. And so we might go on drawing contrasts, distinctions, differences. . . . The central figure in all the documents is Jesus, but how variously he is described. Now — and this was apparently his own favourite name for himself — he is " the Son of man "; now he is " the Servant of God " (Acts); now he is " the second Adam " (Paul); now he is " the eternal High-priest after the order of Melchizedek " (Hebrews); now he is " the *Logos* incarnate " (John). And if the Saviour is so variously described, no less so are the saved People: " the followers of the Way," " the brethren," " the saints," " the elect," " the remnant," " the body of Christ," and so forth.

It is on such differences that analytical criticism concentrates; it reveals contrasts, divergencies, inconsistencies; it distinguishes the various christologies, soteriologies, eschatologies in the New Testament and labels them Synoptic, Pauline, Petrine, Johannine, and so on. Small wonder then that the plain man is perplexed and wonders wistfully which particular brand of New Testament theology has the best claim to be accounted truly Christian. Nor is the expert always of much help to him. In his zeal for analysis the expert isolates a portion of the New Testament for microscopic study — the Synoptic Gospels, or the Pauline *corpus* perhaps — and too often fails to reveal the connexions of his particular study with the rest of the New Testament. Here, as elsewhere, " isolationism " involves dangers; it leads to a piecemeal treatment of early Christian thought; it makes men propound unreal dilemmas, like " Jesus or Paul? "; it produces " Gospel scholars," " Paulinists," " Johannine authorities," excellent men all, but men ever in danger of not seeing the wood for the particular trees on which their gaze is focused. Only the greatest masters in Biblical criticism and interpretation, men whose understanding is not of the Synoptic Gospels only, or Paul, or " John," but of the whole New Testament, see things in their proper perspective and have an eye for the unity that underlies all diversity. "It needs the *whole* of the New Testament," said one of them, " to show what Christ is." [1]

One chief task before New Testament scholarship is therefore to lay bare this unity. It is a task of capital importance; for it really raises the question: What is the meaning and message of the New Testament? and until we arrive at a rough answer to it, we shall never fully understand the individual documents. The New Testament resembles a great jig-saw puzzle composed of many and various pieces. Hitherto we have pored over the pieces in isolation and largely failed to see the picture. But now, piece after piece is slowly falling into its proper place and helping to make the whole pattern luminous.

Let me put on record my own experience. When I began serious study of the New Testament, Liberal criticism, despite several heavy frontal attacks upon it, still held the field. Much has happened in criticism, as in the world, since then; and the Liberals are now fighting a defensive battle. Indeed it is the fashion nowadays in some quarters to dismiss them with derision. Such derision is at once ungracious and ungrateful: ungracious because few of us are entitled to speak disrespectfully of undoubted masters like Adolf Harnack; ungrateful, because it forgets the immense debt we all owe in New Testament criticism to the work of great Liberal scholars: indeed, without their labours — and their errors — we could not properly see our task to-day. Nevertheless I must confess that the Liberals left me with not a few unsolved problems. To take one obvious example: if the Liberal conception of Jesus and the Gospel was the whole truth, then Paul and all his successors were wrong; for the Liberal Jesus, sublime and attractive figure as he was, was a lay figure quite incapable of creating apostolic Christianity. On the Liberal view, Paul (or, on Bousset's view,[2] some pre-Pauline Christians living in a Hellenistic *milieu*) was the " gratuitous sophisticator " who spoiled everything; it was he who changed the idyll of Galilee into a cosmic drama of redemption; it was he, in short, who really substituted a complicated religion *about* Jesus for an original and simple religion *of* Jesus.

All this is familiar and even trite. . . . What I wish to say is that with the eclipse of the Liberal interpretation under the influence of Schweitzer and others and with the new light shed on the eschatology of the Gospels, much that was dark has become luminous. To come down for a moment to particulars, our new understanding of the eschatological character of the Kingdom of God in the Synoptic Gospels, of great Pauline conceptions such as "in Christ" and "the righteousness of God," of the content of the earliest apostolic preaching — all this has paved the way for a new approach to the New Testament, in which its essential unity shines out ever more clearly.

The older approach was analytical; the newer approach will be synthetic. The older approach revealed variety; the newer approach will disclose unity amid that variety. Here another example will make the point clear. The Synoptic

Gospels speak of the advent of " the Kingdom of God ";
Paul of " being in Christ ", John of " the Logos becoming
incarnate." Now, isolate each of these phrases, and observe what is likely to happen. Your study of the Kingdom of God may take you back through Judaism to the
Old Testament and perhaps even (as it did Otto) to primitive Aryan religion. Your study of the Pauline formula
" in Christ " may take you back to Hellenistic mysticism
(as it did Deissmann). Your study of the *Logos* may take
you back through Philo to Plato and the Stoics. At the
end of your investigations you may be left wondering what
conceivable connexion there is among them all. Yet when
Jesus said, " The Kingdom of God has come upon you "
(Luke x. 9) and Paul " If any man is in Christ, there is a
new creation " (2 Cor. v. 17) and John " The *Logos* became flesh and dwelt among us " (John i. 14), they were
not making utterly different and unrelated announce-
ments; on the contrary, they were using different idioms,
different categories of thought, to express their common
conviction that the living God had spoken and acted
through his Messiah for the salvation of his people: in
fine, they were setting forth, each in a pregnant phrase,
the one *Heilsgeschichte.*

NOTE ON THE EQUIVALENCE OF CERTAIN CARDINAL NEW TESTAMENT EXPRESSIONS

The Synoptic Gospels treat of " the Gospel of the Kingdom (of God)" (*e.g.* Matt. iv. 23); St. Paul of " the Gospel
of Christ " (Rom. xv. 19); St. John of " the Word of life "
(1 John i. 1). So far as words go, they all appear to be
speaking of different things. But it is not really so.

Consider the Synoptics. Here the Kingdom (or redemptive Rule) of God and the person of Christ are inex-

tricably bound up with each other. Jesus incarnates the redemptive Rule of God: " if I (ἐγώ : emphatic) by the finger of God cast out demons," Jesus said, " then is the Kingdom of God come upon you " (Luke xi. 20; Q). Further, to be a disciple of Jesus is to be " in the Kingdom." " The Kingdom is promised only to those that attach themselves to his person " (P. T. Forsyth, *The Person and Place of Jesus Christ,* p. 108). So close is the connexion between Jesus and the Kingdom that the *dictum* of Marcion (for even heretics often stumble on the truth!) is entirely justified: " In the Gospel the Kingdom of God is Christ himself." *The Kingdom is Christ.*

Consider St. Paul. Paul's equivalent for " the Kingdom of God has come upon you (in the person of Jesus) " is " the righteousness of God (*i.e.* God's redeeming activity, a synonym for ' salvation '[3]) has been manifested," namely, in Christ (see Rom. iii. 21 ff.). Further, for Paul to preach the Gospel is to preach Christ. A comparison of two famous passages will show this:

" I am not ashamed of *the Gospel;* for it is *the power of God* unto salvation to everyone that believeth; to the Jew first and also to the Greek " (Rom. i. 16). " We preach Christ crucified, unto Jews a stumbling-block and unto Gentiles foolishness; but unto them that are called, both Jews and Greeks, Christ *the Power of God* and the wisdom of God " (1 Cor. i. 23 f.). *The Gospel is Christ.*

Consider St. John. " Life " or " eternal Life " is the dominant idea in his writings. Where the Synoptists speak of " the Kingdom," John speaks of " eternal Life." But for John this supreme blessing is so bound up with Christ that (with true interpretation) he can represent Jesus as saying: " I am the Life " (John xi. 25, xiv. 6; cf. also vi. 35, 48). *The Life is Christ;* or, as John himself says (1 John v. 11), "This Life is in his Son."

Thus we shall not stray far from the truth if in reading the New Testament we make the following equations:

(1) The Gospel of the Kingdom = the Gospel of Christ = the Word of Life.

(2) To be " in the Kingdom " = to be " in Christ " = to have " eternal Life." [4]

NOTES

[1] Denney. See his *Letters to W. Robertson Nicoll*, p. 20.

[2] In *Kyrios Christos*.

[3] See C. H. Dodd, *Romans*, pp. 9–13.

[4] An examination of Mark x. 17–31 permits the following rough equation:

To follow Jesus = to inherit eternal life = to enter the Kingdom of God = to be saved.

CHAPTER THREE

CRITICAL CONSIDERATIONS

AFTER OUTLINING our aim as a search for the unity underlying the diversity of the New Testament we turned aside to discuss the inadequacy of the analytical approach to it. Now we must proceed to an exposition of the " more excellent way." We may call it " the synthetic approach." Believing that those who gathered the New Testament documents into a canon discovered in them, in spite of all diversities, a deep unity of theme, we must try to show wherein that unity consists.

But before we plunge *in medias res,* one or two critical and other observations fall to be made.

Since there is no intention to write a complete theology of the New Testament from the synthetic point of view, we shall make a representative selection of the documents and by appeal to these try to prove our case. Our selection is as follows: The Synoptic Gospels; Acts; the Pauline Epistles (except the Pastorals which are non-Pauline in their extant form); First Peter; Hebrews; and the Gospel and First Epistle of St. John. The selection, we claim, embraces the chief types of New Testament Christianity. The only important documents omitted (except the Pastorals) are the Epistle of James and Revelation. Of the Epistle we may say, while not wholly endorsing Luther's famous judgment on it, that the Epistle of James contains little that is specifically Christian [1] — our Lord's name occurs but twice in it — except its healthy moral tone so reminiscent in places of the Sermon on the Mount. The

Apocalypse we might have used; but this book despite its occasional splendours of imagination and expression is in many respects (its eschatology, its conception of God, its picture of the Messiah) more Jewish than Christian, and may therefore for our purpose be excluded.

On the selected documents two further remarks are needed. First, we may accept (with most British scholars) the common authorship of the Fourth Gospel and the First Epistle of St. John; the latter being perhaps designed as a covering letter to the Gospel (Lightfoot), or maybe written later as an appeal to the Church to abide by the spiritual teaching of the Gospel (Brooke).

Second, remembering that Silvanus was the actual writer (1 Pet. v. 12) we may reasonably assume (with most British scholars) that St. Peter's authority stands behind the first epistle bearing his name: " the voice may well be Peter's voice, though the literary hand may have been the hand of Silvanus." [2]

Since we shall have occasion to study our documents in their chronological order, a table of approximate dates may here be added:

St. Paul's Epistles .	50–60
First Peter	c. 67
The Synoptic Gospels .	65–85
Hebrews .	c. 80
The Fourth Gospel and First Epistle of St. John [3] .	90–100

We are now ready to " clap into it roundly." In the light of what was said at the outset, three main approaches call for exploration.

The first we may call Christological; it will deal with the *kerygma* of the New Testament and with the Person who is the subject of the *kerygma:* " we preach *Christ*" (κηρύσσομεν Χριστόν, 1 Cor. i. 23).

The second will take us into the realm of ecclesiology; it will deal with the Church as the People of God.

The third will deal with New Testament soteriology. —salvation

But all these are so closely connected that one implies the other — and all lead to the one centre, the *Heilsgeschichte*. It is a trinity in unity.

NOTES

1 Cf. Lake (*Introduction to the New Testament,* p. 164): " Perhaps the most Jewish book in the New Testament, its only possible rival for that distinction being the Apocalypse."

2 MacNeile, *N.T. Teaching in the Light of St. Paul's,* p. 136.

3 By " John " in the sequel I mean the Fourth Evangelist (who is, in my judgment, John the Elder).

I. One Lord

CHAPTER FOUR

THE KERYGMA

IN OUR FIRST APPROACH we are concerned with a message of salvation which centres in a Saviour. But for the sake of clearness we shall treat these two — the message and the Saviour — separately.

The message of salvation is what the New Testament calls *kerygma.* Let us dwell a moment on the word itself. *Keryssein,* from which it is derived, is one of the great verbs in the New Testament. It occurs some sixty-one times: Matthew (9), Mark (14), Luke (9), Acts (8), Paul (17), Pastorals (2); 1 Peter (1), Revelation (1).[1] It is the verb which Jesus used to describe his mission (Mark i. 38; Luke iv. 18 f.); which describes the work of his twelve " envoys " (Mark vi. 12); which describes the function of the earliest Christian missionaries (*e.g.* Rom. x. 14). What does it mean? *Keryssein* means to perform the office of a *keryx* or " herald," to PROCLAIM with authority to all and sundry a message with which one has been entrusted. In our translations of the New Testament the word is normally rendered " preach "; but the associations which have gathered around our word " preaching " may easily mislead us as to the true meaning of *keryssein*. In the New Testament the verb does not mean " to give an informative or hortatory or edifying discourse expressed in beautifully arranged words with a melodious voice; it means *to proclaim an event* "[2]; and that event the coming of God's redemptive Rule in Jesus Christ.

24

From the verb comes the noun *kerygma*. It may signify either the act of proclamation or the thing proclaimed. The first sense occurs in 1 Cor. ii. 4: " my language and my *kerygma*," says Paul, " were not armed with the persuasive words of wisdom but with the convincing power of the Spirit." But in the New Testament the second meaning is commoner: the *kerygma* is the thing — the event — proclaimed.

Thus, in the shorter ending of St. Mark, " Jesus sent forth through them (the Apostles) the sacred and incorruptible *kerygma* of eternal salvation "; or in Paul, " It pleased God through the foolishness of the *kerygma* to save them that believe " (1 Cor. i. 21); " If Christ has not been raised, then is our *kerygma* vain " (1 Cor. xv. 14); " according to my gospel and the *kerygma* of Jesus Christ " (Rom. xvi. 25). In these passages the emphasis falls on the *content* of the *kerygma*. That content can be expressed in the two words of the last quotation — Jesus Christ. No doubt it is true that in 1 Cor. i. 21 Paul is thinking primarily of Christ *crucified* — the " scandal " of the Cross which offends alike the Jews in their demand for " signs " and the Greeks in their quest for wisdom; while in 1 Cor. xv. 14 Paul's main concern is with " Christ *risen* from the dead." Yet always, " the thought is of the *whole* Christ, who through death and resurrection has become the Lord and is preached as such (2 Cor. iv. 5). The earthly and the exalted One cannot be separated." [3]

Kerygma, therefore, in its usual New Testament signification and in the sense in which we use it, means the proclaimed message of salvation. It is practically synonymous with *euangelion,* " gospel." It is a proclamation containing " good news," the good news of an event, *the* event, the saving Act of God in Jesus Christ, whereby " He has visited and redeemed his people." As such, *kerygma* is to be distinguished from *didache* which denotes moral and spiritual instruction for those who have already accepted the *kerygma*. (The first Epistle to the Corinthians is a good example of *didache;* so, at a later date, is *The Teaching (didache) of the Twelve Apostles.*)

Having defined our term, we must now proceed to a fuller exposition of its contents in the New Testament.

"Preaching (i.e. *kerygma*)," says Martin Dibelius, "was the original seat of all tradition about Jesus." [4] This is probably an overstatement; and we should put a query after the word "all." [5] Nevertheless there is substantial truth in the contention of Dibelius and other "Form-critics," that (if we may so phrase it) "in the beginning was the *kerygma*." Long before any of our written gospels appeared, even before St. Paul began to write his epistles, the apostles and their coadjutors were proclaiming the *kerygma* or message of salvation. It is this suggestion that Professor C. H. Dodd has elaborated in *The Apostolic Preaching and its Developments* which must rank as one of the most important and positive contributions to New Testament science in our generation. The outline of that *kerygma* we can reconstruct from fragments of early Christian tradition embedded in St. Paul's epistles and reflected in the early speeches of Acts.

The chief passages in St. Paul's epistles are: Rom. i. 2–5 (which reads like a credal fragment and contains un-Pauline features [6]); Rom. iv. 24–25 [7]; Rom. x. 8–9; 1 Cor. xv. 3 ff. (which Paul expressly calls "tradition" which he had "received"). Other probable passages are: Rom. viii. 31–4; 1 Thess. i. 9–10; and Gal. i. 3–4.

Our other source for the *kerygma* is the early speeches of Acts. Although we may not regard these speeches as preserving the precise words of Peter, several considerations make it probable that they enshrine early Christian tradition.

First, Luke (who is, in my judgment, the author of Luke-Acts) seems often to have used sources, or personal recollections, when he composed the speeches in Acts, and not to have freely invented. The speech to the Ephesian Elders at Miletus (Acts xx. 18–35), so full of Pauline traits, is the clearest example. Second, these early speeches in Acts attributed to Peter not only sound " primitive " but betray little or nothing of St. Paul's influence. Third, without accepting *in toto* Torrey's theory[8] that Acts i.–xv. is based on a single Aramaic document, it is hard to resist the conclusion that Luke in these early chapters of Acts largely depends on Aramaic sources.

The chief speeches in question are as follows:

Acts ii. 14–39: Speech on Day of Pentecost.
   " iii. 12–26: Speech at Solomon's Porch.
   " iv. 8–12: Speech to Sanhedrin.
   " x. 36–43: Speech to Cornelius.

The case for an Aramaic original is perhaps strongest in the last speech. The Greek of it almost defies translation. Yet Luke, the writer of Acts, is the best Grecian — excepting perhaps the unknown author of Hebrews — among the New Testament writers. If, however, with Torrey, we put it back into Aramaic, it becomes tolerably perspicuous. It is therefore reasonable to infer that Luke was wrestling here with an intractable Aramaic source. Since this speech is of special interest, it may be worth while to set it down and to print the parallels from the Pauline *kerygma* alongside it:

Acts x. 36–43	The *Kerygma* in Paul
The word which He sent to the sons of Israel	The good-news of God . . . concerning His Son . . . Jesus Christ
Preaching good news of peace [9] through Jesus Christ (He is Lord of all) —	our Lord (Rom. i. 2–4)
You know the matter that came to pass through all Judæa, beginning from Galilee, after the baptism which John preached (concerning) Jesus of Nazareth. How that God anointed him with Holy Spirit and power,	(cf. Mark i 14) Who was appointed the Son of God with *power* according to *the spirit of holiness* (Rom. i. 4) [10]
Who went about doing good and healing all who were oppressed by the devil, for God was with him. And we are witnesses of all that he did both in the country of the Jews and in Jerusalem,	(cf. 2 Cor. v. 19: God was in Christ)
Whom also they slew by hanging on a TREE	(cf. Gal. iii. 13 (TREE))
Him God raised up on the third day	He hath been raised on the third day (1 Cor. xv. 4). God raised him from the dead (Rom. x. 9)
And gave him to be made manifest; not to all the people but to witnesses pre-elected by God, even us who ate and drank with him after he rose from the dead. And he charged us to preach unto the people and to testify that this is he who is appointed by God Judge of living and dead. To	He appeared (1 Cor. xv. 5 ff.) (cf. the list of select witnesses given in 1 Cor. xv. 5 ff.) (cf. Rom. ii. 16: God shall judge . . . through Jesus Christ (2 Cor. v. 10; 1 Cor. iv. 4 f.))

Acts x. 36–43	The *Kerygma* in Paul
him bear all the prophets witness, that every one believing on him should receive remission of sins through his name.	Which he promised before through his prophets in (the) holy scriptures (Rom. i. 2; cf. also 1 Cor. xv. 3: Christ died for our sins according to the scriptures.)

Thus, comparing the evidence derived from Acts with that from Paul, we can roughly reconstruct the apostolic *kerygma*. Evidently those early Christian sermons had three " heads ":

I. A CLAIM THAT THEIR MESSAGE WAS THE FULFILMENT OF OLD TESTAMENT PROPHECY.

" This is that which hath been spoken by the prophet " (Acts ii. 16) ; " to him bear all the prophets witness " (Acts x. 43) ; " promised before by his prophets in (the) holy scriptures " (Rom. i. 2) ; " according to the scriptures " (1 Cor. xv. 3–4).

2. A HISTORICAL EXPOSITION SETTING FORTH JESUS IN HIS LIFE, DEATH, RESURRECTION, AND EXALTATION (all conceived as one great act of God), which ran as follows:

Jesus, the promised Saviour of the New Age now dawning, was born of David's line (Acts ii. 30; Rom. i. 3); he went about doing good and executing mighty works by God's power in Galilee and Judæa (Acts x. 37 f.); he was crucified on a tree [11] (Acts v. 30, x. 39; Gal. iii. 13) according to God's " settled " purpose (Acts ii. 23) and will revealed in the Scriptures (Acts iii. 18; Rom. iv. 25; 1 Cor. xv. 3); he has been raised by God's power from the dead (Acts ii. 24, 32, iii. 15, etc.; 1 Cor. xv. 4, etc.), and is exalted to his right hand (Acts ii. 33; Rom. viii. 34). He will come again as Judge and Saviour (Acts iii. 20 f., x. 42; 1 Thess. i. 10; Rom. ii. 16).

3. A SUMMONS TO REPENT AND ACCEPT THE FORGIVENESS OF SINS IN JESUS (Acts ii. 38, iii. 19, x. 43).

Such, then, was the *kerygma* of the earliest preachers. Whether they spoke of preaching the Kingdom of God or of preaching Christ — such in substance was their Gospel.

But — and here is the bearing of our discussion on the problem of unity — this *kerygma* which we have recovered from Paul and Acts *runs through the whole New Testament;* like a song which keeps sounding in our heads in all sorts of circumstances, we hear again and again the authentic notes of the *kerygma* ring out in gospel, epistle, and homily.

We start with the Gospels. In what literary category are we to place them? Whatever hard things we may say of the Form-critics, we must own that they have compelled us to face that question and pointed us to the true answer. The evangelists are not biographers, nor are the Gospels biographies. We search vainly in the Gospels for the things which any competent biographer supplies: details about the early years and education, the personal appearance and characteristics of his hero; specific notes of time and place in the story of the celebrity's life; a psychological attempt to unravel motives of action and to trace out his developing consciousness of the life-work which gives him a place in history. Of all these the Gospels tell us next to nothing.

If not biographies, what, then, are the Gospels? The answer, briefly put, is that they are expanded forms of the *kerygma* which we have just been studying. " The Gospels," says K. L. Schmidt, " in their literary peculiarity can only be explained from the early Christian *kerygma* as it is found both in the speeches of Acts and the Pauline letters." [12]

Consider the earliest Gospel, St. Mark. Put St. Mark in its broad outline side by side with the apostolic *kerygma* as it occurs in what has been called its *locus classicus*, [13] Acts x. 36–43 (Peter's speech to Cornelius), and you will see that our earliest Gospel is simply an expanded form of the *kerygma* (the emphasis being, of course, on " the historical section ").

St. Mark's Gospel opens, as the *kerygma* opens, with the fulfilment of prophecy (Mark i. 2 f.). As in Acts x. 37, all began " in Galilee after the baptism which John preached," so St. Mark begins his narrative on the banks of Jordan and proceeds to relate how Jesus came into Galilee announcing the advent of the Kingdom (Mark i. 14 f.). The ensuing chapters in Mark (i. 16–viii.) are an illustrative expansion of the *kerygma's* declaration: " who went about doing good, and healing all that were oppressed by the devil; for God was with him " (Acts x. 38). Then, as in Acts x., Mark's narrative goes on to recount Jesus' doings " both in the country of the Jews and in Jerusalem." The amount of space Mark devotes to the Passion and the events that led up to it (viii. 31–xv. 47) corresponds to the emphasis on the Cross in the *kerygma* of Acts and Paul. Finally, after recording the death of Jesus, Mark proceeds to relate, as the *kerygma* did (1 Cor. xv. 4), that " he was buried and that he hath been raised on the third day." The end of Mark's Gospel is lost. Doubtless the evangelist went on to record an appearance (or appearances) of the risen Jesus. But whatever the tenor of the lost ending, we have enough to show what the climax of the story was. Surely it is clear that in composing his gospel Mark was following the pattern of the *kerygma* — retelling for the benefit of his Roman readers, and with the help of many anecdotes received from Peter and others, the same story of God's saving activity in Jesus his Messiah which was the theme of all the apostolic preachers.

We shall now briefly consider St. Matthew and St. Luke in terms of the *kerygma*. Since the writers of both our first and third gospels used St. Mark as their basis or framework,[14] they, too, reflect the pattern of the *kerygma*. But the pattern is not so clear as in St. Mark; for in St. Matthew and St. Luke the *kerygma* has, so to speak, been mixed with *didache,* namely, " Q," and the special teaching preserved in the special sources which we call " M " and " L." The inclusion of this new material inevitably blurs somewhat the outline of the *kerygma*. Nevertheless, in certain respects St. Matthew and St. Luke underline elements in the *kerygma* which do not stand out clearly in St. Mark. One is the Davidic descent of Jesus. The genealogies in St. Matthew and St. Luke are inserted to attest this fact. Another element is the appeal to the fulfilment of the Old Testament in Jesus which is so conspicuous a feature in St. Matthew. Many of the First Evangelist's proof-texts seem to us forced and artificial: but our impatience of such proof-texts should not blind us to the deeper truth which the Evangelist is seeking to convey — that in the life, death, and resurrection of Jesus the Messianic hope of the Old Testament was fulfilled. And that, of course, simply represents the first section of the apostolic *kerygma*.

Does the Fourth Gospel reflect the *kerygma*? Most certainly; the pattern of the *kerygma* stands out more clearly in the Fourth Gospel than in St. Matthew and St. Luke. The *kerygma* opened, as we have seen, with a claim that in Jesus the Messiah the prophecies were fulfilled. Where can we trace this in St. John? Obviously, in the Prologue: the *Logos* or Word of the Lord which originally wrought in the Creation of all things (Gen. i.), which shone unconquerably amid man's spiritual darkness in bygone days, which in the prophets struggled for expression — " coming home " to God's people, albeit his " own folk " received him not — this Word has now at last been embodied in human flesh, and the Old Testament is fulfilled.

There follows, as in the *kerygma,* the Ministry of the Baptist. As in Acts x. and in St. Mark, so in the Fourth Gospel, Jesus at his Baptism is the " anointed of the Spirit." Thereafter John recapitulates the familiar stages in the *kerygma:* Jesus' teaching and miracles in Galilee, his ministry in Judæa and Jerusalem, the Trial, Crucifixion, Burial, and the Resurrection. The *kerygma* survives; but it is profoundly restated, notable in two directions: (1) The Second Advent of Christ conceived by the earliest preachers in apocalyptic terms now becomes in the " sublimated eschatology " of John a Return in the person of his *alter ego,* the Holy Spirit (John xiv. 16–19, xvi. 12–16). (2) The Last Judgment, which in the earliest *kerygma* lay in the (probably very near) future is now regarded as having in some sense come with the coming of Christ (John iii. 19, xii. 31).

Thus far we have found the *kerygma* in Paul and Acts and in the Four Gospels. Our argument will be complete if we can now find the *kerygma* in the two remaining documents in our list, First Peter and Hebrews.

It is one of the arguments in favour of the apostolic authorship of First Peter that a primitive atmosphere informs this document. At all events, the notes of the earliest preaching ring out very plainly in it.

" The prophecies are fulfilled in the Gospel " is the

meaning of those rather difficult verses, ch. i. 10–12. We might paraphrase them thus to make the meaning clearer:

" It was nothing but this hope of salvation which mightily exercised the prophets of old. They strove to learn when and how would be fulfilled those mysterious things to which the spirit of the Messiah, speaking in them, pointed. That spirit spoke of the Messiah's sufferings and the glories to follow them. They knew, these olden prophets, that these things would be fulfilled not in their own generation but in some blessed future one. And that fulfilment you now enjoy in the Gospel."

That Gospel, so St. Peter goes on to say in his letter, centres in Jesus the Messiah who died to redeem his People (i. 18 f.) and whose suffering and death for sin on the tree accorded with the divine purpose as revealed in the scriptures (ii. 21–24; Isa. liii.; Deut. xxi. 22). He was raised from the dead by God's power (i. 3, 21, iii. 21); and exalted to God's right hand (iii. 22). The Last Judgment is imminent (iv. 5, 17).

Last of all, let us look for the *kerygma* in Hebrews. The theme of the fulfilment of prophecy rings out in the opening verses: God who " in many fragments and in many modes " revealed himself to old Israel through the Prophets has now at this turning-point of history revealed himself to us in his Son. All the strands of the Messianic hope, the writer would say, are gathered up and embodied in him. Not even John has expressed the idea of the fulfilment of the Old Testament in Jesus more sublimely.

Then, as we proceed throught the epistle, we find the writer, though he is chiefly concerned to depict Jesus as the Ideal High Priest, betraying again and again his knowledge of the *kerygma*. Thus in vii. 14 he asserts (in effect) the Davidic descent of Jesus: " He sprang of Judah "; he refers to the original preaching of this " so great salvation " by the Lord Jesus (ii. 3); and he recurs many times in the course of his high argument to the life and mission of Jesus. Once (ii. 5 ff.) he almost calls Jesus " the Son of Man "; he speaks repeatedly of the suffering and temptation Jesus had known; he finds the ruling principle of Jesus' life in his obedience to God's will (v. 8, x. 7). His death on the Cross (xii. 2) for sin, " outside the gate " (xiii. 12), was according to God's purpose: the writer's equivalent for " by the determinate counsel of God " (Acts ii. 23) appearing in v. 1 ff. with its emphasis on Jesus' " appointment " by God (cf. also ii. 9–10).

He was raised by God's power from the dead (xiii. 20); exalted to " the right hand of the Majesty on high " (i. 3, 13, viii. 1, x. 12, xii. 2); and will come again (ix. 28, x. 25 ff., x. 37, etc.) for judgment.

It is the same *kerygma* which we have found in all our documents; but once again it is restated — this time in terms of the Platonic doctrine of the two worlds. Thus, for example, the death of Christ is here interpreted as his passage into the eternal order (ix. 12, 24).

To sum up. We are in quest of unity in the New Testament; and here in the *kerygma* we have found an excellent example of it. Through the variegated fabric of the New Testament now clear and conspicuous, now veiled and hidden, runs the golden thread of the *kerygma*. Years ago, P. T. Forsyth perceived this when he wrote: " There was no universal theological formula, there was not an orthodoxy, but certainly there was a common apostolic gospel, a *kerygma*." [15] And was not Paul making the same point when he wrote: " Whether then it be I or they, so we preach and so you believed " (1 Cor. xv. 11)?

We may conclude this study of the *kerygma* in the New Testament on a practical note. What does it mean to preach the Gospel to-day? Obviously, any presentation of the Christian Faith in the twentieth century which claims to be truly Christian must bear a real relation to the preaching of the first apostles. If that be so, preaching which finds the heart of the Gospel in, say, The Fatherhood of God, or the ethical principles of the Sermon on the Mount, must be regarded not as unchristian, but as a failure to "continue steadfastly in the apostles' doctrine" (Acts ii. 42). It is *didache;* but it is not *kerygma.* Not primarily in these terms did the apostles preach. Any preaching to-day which aims to be in line with the original Gospel must conserve the essential affirmations of the Apostolic preaching. Its core and kernel will be a story — a story that sounds as crazy to many of our wise men to-day as it did to the Greeks of Paul's day — a story centring in a Jew called Jesus the Messiah in whom the prophecies made of old to Israel were fulfilled, in whose life, death, resurrection, and exaltation the Living God acted conclusively for us men and our salvation; and in the experience of whose followers, *i.e.* the Church, there was revealed a new quality of life, arising out of what God had done, which in turn confirmed the value set on the saving facts in the story.

But that story will have to be restated in terms intelligible to modern men and women for whom the technical terms of Jewish eschatology — the conceptions of the Kingdom and the Messiah and of the Two Ages — mean little or nothing. The argument from the fulfilment of Scripture is still valid; but if it is to carry conviction to-day, it cannot be presented as St. Matthew presented it or as our forefathers who lived before the days of Higher Criticism presented it. (See A. G. Hebert's recent book, *The Throne of David:* a study of the Fulfilment of the Old Testament in Jesus Christ and His Church, which is a praiseworthy attempt to restate the argument.) Of course, all such restatement is exposed to danger — the danger that in the process of making the primitive Gospel acceptable and relevant to the men of to-day something essential may be lost. In that case we shall run the risk of "preaching another Jesus and another Gospel." But the same task of restatement confronted the apostles and their successors — Paul, John, the writer to the Hebrews, etc. — when they set themselves to commend the truth of the Gospel to the great Gentile world. How nobly they succeeded, the Epistle to the Romans, the Fourth Gospel, and the Epistle to the Hebrews bear witness. Such works should serve as an abiding incentive and summons to us to do for our generation what they so magnificently did for theirs.

There is one point more which in our preoccupation with the discovery of the primitive *kerygma* we may easily forget. A great preacher once defined preaching as the communication of " truth through personality." Before our preaching of the gospel can be with power it must become a personal possession, and so be uttered with a personal signature. How often Paul in one way or another speaks of " my gospel." This gospel was not something of his own inventing. The kernel of it was something which he had received. But it was nevertheless also truly his own. It had passed through the alembic of his own mind and been proven true in his own experience. In short, the gospel he preached was at once old and new, at once something which he had received and something indefeasibly his own.

So, too, it must be with our presentation of the Apostolic Gospel. Perhaps an illustration will make the point better than any number of arguments. Nearly forty years ago the building committee of Liverpool Cathedral issued an advertisement inviting the submission of portfolios of drawings. Out of one hundred and three portfolios submitted, five were approved, and their senders recommended to submit designs for a new Cathedral. Of these five designs one was more excellent than the rest. Giles

Gilbert Scott, lately come of age, designed Liverpool Cathedral, that triumph of architecture. And yet behind that story of Liverpool Cathedral lies the story of all other great cathedrals. All the art and craft of masons, all the skill of workers in wood and glass and bronze, all the needs of a worshipping community accumulated over hundreds of years guided Scott's pen as he wrought out his great design. "What I delivered unto you I first of all myself received," is the golden rule of architecture as well as of preaching. And yet not a stone of that vast fabric but bears the impress of Scott's genius. It was he that set it in its appointed place — that architrave — that plinth — that shafted flight of stone. "My cathedral," might Giles Gilbert Scott well say: and so, "my Gospel."

The Christian preacher, if he is to be loyal to his commission, must preach the Apostolic Gospel; but first he must make it his own.

NOTES

1 It does not occur in the Fourth Gospel or Johannine Epistles. John prefers μαρτυρεῖν.

2 Friedrich in *Kittel's Th. Wb. sub. κηρύσσω*.

3 Friedrich, *op. cit.*

4 *From Tradition to Gospel*, p. 14.

5 See V. Taylor, *The Gospels*, p. 20.

6 See my book, *Paul and his Predecessors*, pp. 25–30.

7 *Ibid.*, 33 f.

8 *The Composition and Date of Acts*.

9 "Peace" = salvation. Cf. Isa. liii. 5; Ps. lxxxv. 8; Eph. vi. 15.

10 Probably a reference to the Baptism of Jesus.

11 This reference to hanging on a *tree* (cf. Deut. xxi. 22) must be part of the primitive *kerygma*.

12 *Theologische Blätter*, May 1931.

13 Ryder Smith, *The Bible Doctrine of Salvation*, p. 202.

14 This statement, as it affects St. Luke, would need to be qualified if the Proto-Luke theory were finally established.

15 *The Principle of Authority*, p. 141.

CHAPTER FIVE

KYRIOS JESUS

or

ONE ESSENTIAL CHRISTOLOGY

OUR FIRST APPROACH to the unity of the New Testament we called christological. Having said this we proceeded to an exposition of the *kerygma* in the New Testament. This was not an adroit changing of the subject. "We preach *Christ*," says St. Paul. At the heart of the *kerygma* lies the first and fundamental Christological affirmation: Jesus is the Christ, the Messiah. However, it was impossible then to deal with the New Testament doctrine of the Christ at any length. This chapter may therefore be regarded as an appendix to that on the *kerygma*. Its aim is to show that one *essential* Christology runs through the New Testament; to prove that however different their language and thought-forms — and these inevitably vary with the particular writer and the particular audience to whom he addresses himself — the New Testament writers exhibit *one common religious attitude to Jesus;* in other words, while holding fast his humanity, they one and all "put him with God"; or, to express it ever more simply, for one and all "Jesus is Lord."

Let us hear the witnesses one by one in chronological order:

1. How did the Primitive Church regard Jesus? Their attitude to him we may learn from certain pre-Pauline phrases in St. Paul's letters and from the early speeches in

Acts. As to the latter, there is no need to reiterate that these speeches preserve early tradition and may be taken to reflect primitive Christian thought about Jesus.[1]   The phrases in St. Paul's letters of special relevance are (1) κύριος Ἰησοῦς (Rom. x. 9), which is almost certainly a pre-Pauline Christian confession of faith and (2) *Maran atha* (1 Cor. xvi. 22) which is probably a watchword of the Aramaic-speaking Mother Church in Jerusalem.

To be sure, these early days must have been a time not so much of theological reflection as of intense religious enthusiasm; and therefore we must not expect from the early believers a fully developed Christology.   Rather, as our sources show, they seized on every title or category available to set forth the significance of their risen and exalted Master: he was, they said, "the Servant of God" (Acts iii. 13, 26, iv. 27–30), or "the Righteous One" (Acts iii. 14), or "the Prophet" (iii. 22 f., vii. 37) whom Moses had foreseen, or "the Pioneer of Life" (iii. 15), or "the Saviour" (Acts v. 31), or even — once — "the Son of Man" (vii. 56).   But the chief point to notice is that while asserting his full humanity — "a man accredited by God" is their phrase (Acts ii. 22) — they believed him to be exalted to God's right hand whence he had poured forth the spirit (ii. 33 f.); he was the One in whose name was the forgiveness of sins (ii. 38, v. 31, x. 43) and who was destined to be the Judge of the living and the dead (x. 42). "Lord and Christ" (ii. 36) — that was how they thought of "the Jesus of history."   The designation "Christ" meant that for them he was the divinely commissioned Deliverer whom God would send to redeem Israel — a person of unique and solitary dignity: there might be many prophets; there could be only one Messiah.   But they also give him the name "Lord" — a Septuagint title for God — and transferred to Jesus words used in the Old Testament of

Jehovah (Acts ii. 21). If anyone remembering the late date of Acts should pronounce the ascription of this latter title to Jesus a probable anachronism, we must point him to that Aramaic phrase *Maran atha* so fortunately preserved for us by St. Paul. That must be an echo of the speech of the Jerusalem Church. Its proper translation is, " Our *Lord,* come! " To translate " Teacher, come! " is obviously inept. The phrase is, in fact, a *prayer* in brief; and it proves, what the story of the dying Stephen confirms (Acts vii. 59), that the earliest believers addressed prayer to Jesus as their exalted Lord. *Lex orandi, lex credendi:* you can tell a man's creed from his prayers. That the Primitive Church could *pray* to *Maran* Jesus, surely shows, what the speeches of Acts declare, that in their thinking these earliest Christians set Jesus on that side of reality which we call divine.

2. St. Paul is our next witness.

Is the attitude of St. Paul to Christ that of the Primitive Church? The answer is an emphatic Yes. We might infer this from the fact that though Paul clashed with the Jerusalem leaders on other issues (*e.g.* table-fellowship: Gal. ii. 11 ff.) there is no evidence that they ever disagreed on the capital issue of Christology. But it will be wiser to see whether the positive evidence supports this argument from silence.

First, however, let us frankly own that Paul greatly enriched Christian thinking about Christ, that he added new christological categories, that he spoke of Christ in ways to which there is no precise parallel in our scanty records of the Primitive Church. Thus, for example, Paul called Christ " the Son," " the second Adam," insisted that " in him dwelleth all the fulness of the Godhead bodily " (Col. ii. 9), linked Christ with the Spirit, and assigned to him not only pre-existence but also a cosmic rôle in creation.

But let us notice two important points: first, in his earliest epistles — those to the Thessalonians, there is nothing, christologically speaking, that really goes beyond the affirmations of the Primitive Church concerning Christ; and, second, if in Colossians, one of his latest epistles, Paul makes christological statements which we cannot parallel in the early chapters of Acts — see especially Col. i. 15-20 — we must remember that he is facing intellectual problems that never came within the horizon of the earliest Christians: in particular, he is writing here with his eye on those Colossian Gnostics who wanted apparently to include Christ in their hierarchy of intermediate intelligences between God and man. Since Paul no less than the earliest Christians believed Christ was the only Saviour, he must needs combat this heresy by showing that Christ's place in the Christian salvation was absolutely central and supreme; and this he does in the christological affirmations of the letter to Colossians. As earlier in his letter to the Galatians when a different situation faced him,[2] so now he says in effect, " Christ is all."

Nevertheless, it remains true that Paul's essential Christology is not fundamentally different from that of the Primitive Church. If both assert the humanity of Jesus (" a man approved by God," says the Primitive Church; " born of a woman," " born under the law," says Paul), for both he is " Lord and Christ "; for both he is exalted to God's right hand; for both he is the destined Judge of quick and dead (Acts x. 42; Rom. ii. 16). It is of him that both say (quoting Joel ii. 32) with " the Day " in view: " whosoever shall call on the name of the Lord shall be saved " (Acts ii. 21; Rom. x. 13). And if the Primitive Church can say, " There is none other name under heaven given among men whereby we must be saved " (Acts iv. 12), Paul can likewise say, " Other foundation can no man

lay than that which is laid, which is Jesus Christ" (1 Cor.
iii. 11). In short, for both, Jesus stands with God over-
against men, and has absolute significance for faith.

3. Our third witness is Peter. (And if the writer of
1 Peter be not the Apostle, he is one whose outlook is that
of "a primitive Christian.") His Christology, like that of
the Primitive Church, is simple. Christ is "the Chief
Shepherd" (v. 4) or the Stone of Prophecy (ii. 6 ff.) or the
Servant of the Lord (ii. 24). But it is more important now
to observe that though for the author Jesus had once been a
man among men who had faced his accusers with a noble
non-resistance (ii. 23), he is now Lord and Christ (ii. 13,
iii. 15), exalted to God's right hand, above all angels and
authorities (iii. 22), a Being to be named in the same
breath with God and the Holy Spirit (i. 2), the Mediator
between God and his people (i. 21, ii. 5).[3]

4. Our fourth witness is Hebrews. No sensitive reader
can miss the change of atmosphere when he passes from
1 Peter to Hebrews. For though Hebrews is full of the
Old Testament — its main thesis being the superiority of
the New Covenant to the Old — yet the book is the first
attempt to state Christianity in terms of the Platonic philos-
ophy, with its doctrine of the two worlds, the phenomenal
and the real. We are reminded, in short, as we read the
book, not of Jerusalem and Peter, but of Alexandria and
Philo.

The main thesis of the writer (Apollos or his twin-
brother?) is that Christ is the ideal High Priest who offered
the ideal sacrifice in the ideal sanctuary, and so secured
what the Levitical system failed to secure — perfect access
to God for his People. It is chiefly therefore in his rôle of
ideal High Priest that our author portrays Jesus. Yet there
is sufficient in his homily to show how he conceived of him
christologically.

In some ways his is the most remarkable Christology of all the apostolic writers: remarkable, because in it the extremes meet. On the one hand, Hebrews is the most *humanitarian* of the apostolic writers. No other dwells so emphatically — or shall we say, so movingly? — on the man Jesus (notice that no less than ten times he is called "Jesus" *simpliciter*) who passed through the whole gamut of our human griefs and trials. On the other hand, Hebrews is the most christological of the apostolic writings. No writer soars into higher christological regions in his attempt to set forth the significance of Jesus. The contrast can be seen by comparing two passages: (1) v. 7–8 and (2) i. 2–4.

Many phrases and titles are applied to Jesus in the course of the high argument: thus, he is "the envoy and high priest of our confession" (iii. 1), "the pioneer and perfecter of faith" (xii. 2), "a high priest after the order of Melchizedek" (v. 10), "the Mediator of a new and better Covenant" (ix. 15, xii. 24). But the essential Christology is the same as we found in the Primitive Church, in Paul, and in Peter. If Jesus is one who "in the days of his flesh" was tempted and tried like every man (iv. 15), he is also "the Son" (five times), "the appointed heir of all things" (i. 2), God's agent in creation, "the radiance of his glory," "the impress of his essence,"[4] the sustainer of the life of the universe and the Redeemer (i. 2 f.) who is "the same yesterday, to-day, and for ever" (xiii. 8). How the writer reconciles these two conceptions of Jesus we are not told; nor does the question concern us now. Sufficient to conclude that for this writer Jesus stands on the side of God[5] over-against men, a sinless Being whose redemptive work has "eternal" value, who lives according to the power of an "indissoluble" life (vii. 16) and who can "save to the uttermost" those who "come to God through him" (vii. 25).

5. The next witnesses are the Synoptic evangelists.
What did they think of Jesus? Observe that here we are
not concerned with the testimony of Jesus to himself which
they preserve but with their *own* estimate of him.

For John Mark, our earliest evangelist, Jesus is the Christ
the Son of God. The superscription of his gospel runs:
" the beginning of the Good news of (= about) Jesus
Christ (the Son of God)." The bracketed words are
probably original; [6] yet if they were not genuine, they
would be a true gloss, for they represent the standpoint of
the evangelist. And " Son of God " means plainly a supernatural Being, supernatural in origin, and therefore supernatural in power." [7] " Jesus is the Christ the Son of God "
is the thesis which John Mark sets himself to elaborate.
He is not writing (as Wellhausen observes) *de vita et
moribus Jesus.* He is filling out — by means of illustrative
stories — the *kerygma,* the *kerygma* which told of One in
whom " God's redemptive Rule " was decisively manifested, and who is now in " the highest place that heaven
affords " — at the right hand of God. No other evangelist
has so realistically depicted for us the man Jesus in all his
true humanity; nevertheless Mark regards himself as writing the story of One who was not only the man Jesus but
who was also the supernatural Christ. And though Mark
gives us no theology of the Incarnation, his conception of
Jesus is not essentially different from that of John.[8]

The attitude of St. Matthew (*i.e.* " the Christian rabbi "
who compiled our first Gospel) to Jesus is still clearer.
One point he labours from beginning to end of his book:
Jesus is the Messiah to whom " bear all the prophets witness." If his proof-texts often leave us cold and his refrain
" That it might be fulfilled " irritates us by its monotonous
recurrence, we must not therefore miss their deeper suggestion, which is that " ancient revelation has been consummated at last, and that the consummation is Jesus." [9]

But a glance at two passages in his work — one at the beginning and the other at the end — will make Matthew's own conception of Christ perfectly clear. The first is Matt. i. 23 (Isa. vii. 14), and the important words: Immanuel, *God with us*. That suggests how the evangelist conceived of Jesus. The second passage is Matt. xxviii. 18-20, the charge of the Risen Jesus to his disciples. If these are not genuine words of Jesus as they stand — and few critics would make this claim — they show at least the place Jesus held in Matthew's faith. He is " the Son," a Being to be named beside the Father and the Spirit, a Being entrusted with all authority in heaven and earth, a Being who is present till the end of time with his own.

We turn now to St. Luke. " The Gospel is written by a believer for believers, and therefore assumes the divine character and divine mission of the Person whose life and work it describes." [10] So writes J. M. Creed; and it is not hard to show the truth of his words. No reader of the Third Gospel can doubt that for St. Luke Jesus had once been a man among men. He it is who shows us oftenest " the kneeling Christ." Yet just as certainly does Luke share the common faith of the Church that Jesus is a divine Being. Three brief proofs will suffice: (1) In Luke i. 35 he refers the origination of Jesus to an immediate act of God. (2) Luke alone of the Synoptic evangelists in narrative gives to Jesus the title ὁ κύριος in the days of his flesh. [11] (3) If, as is probably true, Luke has largely shaped the words set in Luke xxiv. 44 ff. on the lips of the risen Jesus, the passage shows us at least what *Luke* thought of Jesus. The Person who is the consummation of all the ancient revelation, the mediator of the forgiveness of sins and the sender of God's Spirit, must stand for the writer on that side of reality which we call divine.

Before we leave the Synoptists, one final observation:

These three evangelists, whom we have been considering, do not represent the attitudes of three *individuals* only; these three gospels were produced in the Church, by the Church, and for the Church. Mark, " Matthew," and Luke are witnesses therefore not only for the individual views of three early Christians, but for the common faith of, shall we say, the Churches in Rome, Antioch, and Cæsarea.

6. Finally, we shall hear the witness of John, as we have it in the Fourth Gospel and First Epistle of John. What place did Jesus hold in the faith of John?

The answer is that the incomparable significance of Jesus for early Christian believers shines out in the Johannine writings with a clarity exceeding anything we have yet found: truly, what first were " points " have now become " stars." [12] Jesus stands for the writer beyond all controversy on that side of reality we call divine. *" Incessu patet deus:* this is indeed the mien of God manifest in the flesh." [13]

But it is wrong to imagine that John is interested only in a divine Being. It is John who in his Gospel tells us of a Jesus who was wearied at Jacob's well (iv. 6), who wept by Lazarus' tomb (xi. 35), who cried " Now is my soul troubled " (xii. 27), and, as he hung on the Cross, " I thirst " (xix. 28). It is John who in his epistle (thinking no doubt of Cerinthus or his like) brands him who denies the reality of the Incarnation as " the master-liar " (ii. 22). The divine Being of whom he writes is the same person who once had been baptized in Jordan and at last had been spiked to a Cross on Calvary. " In no early Christian document," says Burkitt, " is the real humanity of Jesus so emphasized as in the Fourth Gospel." [14]

Yet it is on the other aspect — the divine aspect — that John dwells. Where at the beginning of their gospels Mark had related Jesus to the Baptist, and Matthew to Abraham, and Luke to Adam, John relates Jesus to the eternal Being of God. Jesus is the Son, the only-begotten (iii. 16, etc.), a Being to be bracketed with God himself (John xvii. 3; 1 John i. 3). He is a Being who can say, " I am the Way, the Truth, the Life " (xiv. 6), or " I am the Resurrection and the Life " (xi. 25), or more briefly ἐγώ εἰμι (viii. 24, 28, xiii. 19) " I am " (where the words to be supplied must be " the all decisive personality "); or finally " I and the Father are one " (John x. 30). That in such utterances we have not so much the *ipsissima verba* of Jesus but in large measure the writer's testimony to Jesus given through Jesus' life, is only one more proof of our general thesis — the incomparable significance of Jesus for New Testament faith. For John, as for the rest, Jesus is not one who can be classed with the greatest and best of men, whether hero, saint, or prophet, but one who confronts men in the truth and power and love of the Eternal God — not the man, or even the superman, but the *supernal* man, the Lord from heaven.

To sum up. Despite great differences of thought and phrase and treatment there is one *essential* Christology in the New Testament. Perhaps it can be best summarized in the primitive Christian confession of faith — κύριος Ἰησοῦς, " Jesus is Lord." "There is a unity in all these early Christian books," said James Denney in his greatest book, *Jesus and the Gospel,* "which is powerful enough to absorb and subdue their differences, and that unity is to be found in a common religious relation to Christ, a common debt to him, a common sense that everything in the relations of God and man must be and is determined by him." [15]

This chapter seems to deserve a postscript bearing on our present-day Christianity. The question arises, Do Christian men and women to-day give Christ that place in their faith which the New Testament gives him? Do we believe *in* Christ as the Apostolic men did, or do we merely believe *with* him?

A frank facing of the facts compels the admission that many professing Christians, who would shrink from calling themselves Unitarians, do in fact not yield to Christ the place he held in the faith of the New Testament writers. They believe *with* Christ; they do not really believe *in* him. They would fain make their own the type of religion which Jesus represents; they do not trust themselves to him, for time and eternity, as the first Christians did. For them Christ is the subject, not the object of faith. He is the first Christian, the first true believer in God the Father, the greatest prophet of God's love, the noblest of elder brothers, and so on. In short, he is Leader; he is not, as for the New Testament writers, Lord. They will honour and reverence Jesus; they will not, as the early Christians did, bracket him with God.

Such an attitude to Jesus is a serious declension from the faith of the New Testament. It is not a properly Christian attitude to Jesus. " A Unitarian," said Coleridge, " may be a Christian, but Unitarianism is not Christianity." The true Christian attitude to Jesus, if the New Testament is any criterion, is not that which allows a man to say, " Just a man but what a man! "; it is that which moves him to avow, " In the Holy One of God I find the very Holiness of God."

Happily there are signs abroad that a great change is setting in. We are returning, at any rate in theological circles, to worthier ways of thought concerning Jesus Christ. To this change many causes and factors have contributed — the discrediting of the Liberal view of Jesus and the gospel, the rise of Karl Barth and his friends, and above all, the

growing recognition among men that only such a Saviour
as the New Testament presents is big enough to save a
world given over to the works of the devil and well-nigh
perishing. If thus far this change is most clearly seen in
theological circles, it is spreading slowly also among those
who do not pretend to be theologians; and we may hope
that where our theological leaders are to-day, the rank and
file of Christians will be to-morrow. To leading the mass
of Christian believers into this New Testament attitude to
Christ it is the duty of those who teach the Christian religion to bend all their efforts. Some would say that even
more ought to be attempted; men should be led to a frank
confession that " Christ is God." The wisdom of this, at
any rate as a first step towards a worthier view of Christ,
may be doubted. Men must creep before they walk. The
supreme affirmations of the Christian Church about Christ
may very well wait till men have been won over to the essential thing, which is the New Testament attitude to
Christ:

> None other Lamb, none other Name,
>   None other Hope in heaven or earth or sea,
> None other Hiding-place from guilt and shame,
>   None beside Thee.   [Christina Rossetti.]

NOTES

1 See J. Weiss, *Primitive Christianity,* pp. 9–10. Cf. Schmiedel, *Ency-
clopædia Biblica,* 42: " It is hardly possible not to believe that this Christology of the speeches of Peter must have come from a primitive source."

2 Whether circumcision and the observance of the Mosaic law must
be added to faith in Christ, if one was to be a real Christian.

3 Note especially iii. 15: " Sanctfy in your hearts Christ as Lord."
This is practically Isa. viii. 13: " The Lord of Hosts him shall ye sanc-
tify "; only the word " Christ " is inserted to show who " The Lord " is.
" To anyone familiar with the religion of the O.T. that meant: give
Christ the place of God in your mind and will " (C. A. Scott).

4 Cf. Wisdom vii. 25 f. A Wisdom Christology.

5 In Hebrews he is actually addressed as God (i. 8).

6 See note on Mark i. 1 in C. H. Turner's *St. Mark* (Gore's Commentary).

7 Rawlinson, *St. Mark,* p. li.

8 Cf. Moffatt, *Theology of the Gospels,* p. 12.

9 Denney, *Jesus and the Gospel,* p. 62.

10 *St. Luke,* p. lxxiii.

11 This usage is confined to the portions of the Third Gospel which Streeter calls " Proto-Luke."

12 Browning's *Death in the Desert.*

13 H. R. Mackintosh, *The Person of Jesus Christ,* p. 99.

14 *Gospel History and its Transmission,* p. 233.

15 P. 101.

II. One Church

CHAPTER SIX

JESUS AND THE CHURCH

IN OUR FIRST APPROACH to the unity of the New Testament
the Ariadne's thread in our hand was the *kerygma*
which centred in a Messiah or Saviour. But a Saviour and
a message of Salvation imply a saved People. Our next
approach therefore is by way of the *Ecclesia,* the People of
God. Our aim is to show that however differently the New
Testament writers express themselves, one essential conception of the Church as the People of God pervades the
New Testament.

Nowhere more clearly than in the doctrine of the Church
is seen the truth of our opening contention that recent research is making the unity of the New Testament ever
plainer. In particular, it has discredited two theories which
a generation ago ranked as "dogmas of critical orthodoxy":

(1) That Jesus did not intend to found a new society.

(2) That the various early Christian communities in
Antioch, Corinth, Ephesus, etc., were, in origin, local and
independent religious associations (cf. the Greek guilds)
which later coalesced into a confederation — the Church.[1]

The eclipse of these two "dogmas" has enabled us to
trace ever more clearly the line of connexion that begins
with Jesus and his "little flock" and runs through the
Primitive Church in Jerusalem to the Churches of Paul
and of John. We begin with:

JESUS AND THE CHURCH

Time was when scholars roundly asserted that Jesus never intended to found a new society. Such assertions are less common nowadays, though still heard.[2] We can show in various ways that Jesus by word and action during his Ministry had the foundation of a new people of God in steady view.

In two passages only in the Gospels (Matt. xvi. 18 and xviii. 17) does the word *ecclesia,* " Church," occur. Scholars are more inclined than formerly to account these passages genuine. But since doubt still hangs over them, we shall not use them in arguing our case. Whether Jesus used the Aramaic equivalent of *ecclesia* or no, he undoubtedly set before himself the high purpose of creating a new " People of God."

That phrase at once takes us back into the Old Testament. We shall not understand the New Testament conception of the Church unless we bear constantly in mind the Old Testament doctrine of Israel as the People of God (Qᵉhal Yahweh: in the LXX ἐκκλησία κυρίου) and its later development in the prophetic doctrine of " the Remnant," *i.e.* the eschatological community which should survive God's judgment on disobedient Israel (*ecclesiola in ecclesia*). This doctrine of Israel as the People of God depends in turn on the Hebrew concept of God, the living and redeeming One, Israel's Ruler and King, who had brought Israel out of Egypt with a mighty hand, established a solemn covenant with them, and made of them his peculiar people.

Let us now set out the arguments that Jesus purposed to create a new Israel, a new People of God.

(1) The first argument may be succinctly stated thus: *The Kingdom of God, which lies at the heart of Jesus'*

words and works, necessarily implies a new People of God.

It is a matter of capital importance that we understand the true New Testament meaning of that much-abused phrase, " The Kingdom of God " (ἡ βασιλεία τοῦ θεοῦ). The Kingdom is *not* the Church; but it implies it. If we begin with linguistics, our first assertion must be that the Aramaic word used by Jesus [3] and translated *Basileia,* means primarily " Kingly Rule " (or sovereignty); and since the purpose of God in exercising his Rule is " to visit and redeem his people," we may call it " God's *redemptive* Rule " (or "*saving* Sovereignty "). Indeed, since God's Rule is to be interpreted not in a static but in a dynamic way (as we shall see in a moment) the Gospel phrase " the Kingdom of God " can be best paraphrased as " The redemptive Rule of God in action," [4] " God acting in his redemptive Rule." This Rule is to be interpreted *eschatologically* and *dynamically.*

(A) " Eschatologically." When the Jews of our Lord's time spoke of God's " Kingly Rule " they sometimes used the phrase rabbinically. Thus the rabbis held that a man who obeyed the Law (or *Torah*) " took upon himself the yoke of the divine sovereignty." In that sense no doubt God's Rule or Sovereignty was a present fact. But oftener they used it in a different way. God was indeed King and Sovereign of the world in the *faith* of the pious Jew; but in *fact* he was not acknowledged as such. Amidst the evil and misery of the present the pious Jew dreamed of a blessed time when the living God would finally and decisively manifest his Rule, overthrow all evil, vindicate the right, and show his grace and mercy to his faithful people. In that sense the *Basileia* of God, his redemptive Rule, is an eschatological idea: it is a great hope — nay more, *the* supreme hope — of the future, of the last times.

That hour had now struck and that hope was now being

fulfilled: such was the core of "the good news" which Jesus came preaching.

(B) "Dynamically." If we construe "the saving Sovereignty of God" statically — conceiving the *Basileia* as a "realm" rather than a "rule" — we shall never properly understand the Gospels. For the Jew, God was the *living* and redeeming God, a God who was known by what he did. History was his workshop; on that stage he acted, and judged, and redeemed. He was not "the eternal not ourselves which makes for righteousness" (Matthew Arnold); he was "the great Doer of redeeming things" (H. R. Mackintosh).

It is that dynamic conception of God's character which informs Jesus' words about the advent of his "saving Sovereignty." "The Parables of the Kingdom" compare the *Basileia* to somebody *doing* something or some living power at work — a woman using yeast with vital force in it, a man sowing seed, a dragnet at work, a seed growing secretly but irresistibly; and so on. "The *Basileia* of God," says Jesus (in a saying which Otto [5] has correctly reconstructed and translated), "exercises its force" (Matt. xi. 12; Luke xvi. 16). "If I by the finger of God am casting out demons, then the Kingdom of God has come upon you" (Luke xi. 20; Matt. xii. 28).

Bearing these things in mind we may now return to our argument. According to the Synoptic Gospels the burden of our Lord's preaching was that the *Basileia* of God had come. That means: the decisive hour of history has struck. The living God is signally manifesting his saving sovereignty. God's redemptive rule is now in action.

But God's Rule does not operate in the void. It demands a sphere of rule. It implies a people living under that Rule. It involves the formation of a community. Thus, the *ecclesia* or people of God is the inevitable correlative of the Rule of God. "The Church is, because the *Basileia* is." [6]

This being so, we are not surprised to find that although the primary meaning of *Basileia* is "Rule," the meaning "sphere of rule" is uppermost in certain sayings of Jesus: "It is good for thee to *enter* into the *Basileia* of God with one eye rather than having two eyes to be cast into hell" (Mark ix. 47). "The publicans and the harlots *go into* the *Basileia* of God before you" (Matt. xxi. 31; [7] cf. also Luke vii. 28, xvi. 16).

Furthermore, certain parables suggest that Jesus envisaged the formation of a community. Conspicuous among these is the Parable of the Mustard Seed (Mark iv. 30–32) which grows until "it puts out great branches, so that the birds of the heaven can lodge under the shadow thereof." Read in the light of the Old Testament passages (Dan. iv. 12; Ezek. xxxi. 3, 6) which these words echo, the parable clearly envisages a community. [8]

But we can go farther. As we have seen, the Redemptive Rule of God centres in Jesus. He is its focal point. He is the Rule of God incarnate. He is "the Kingdom." Where he speaks and works, the saving Sovereignty of God is mightily present and active. If, then, he calls men to follow him, if he summons men to personal attachment to himself, then the Redemptive Rule of God is, through him, creating its sphere of rule, is forming the little company of those who live under God's Rule, is gathering together, albeit in tiniest nucleus, the People of God. This finds its confirmation in the obvious fact that in the Gospels to be a disciple of Jesus is to be "in the Kingdom." [9]

Our first argument therefore stands: the Redemptive Rule of God which Jesus proclaimed as a present and dynamic reality, involves the gathering of a new people of God.

(2) Closely related to the first argument is the second, which may be briefly expressed thus: *the idea of Messiah-ship, as Jesus interpreted it, implies the gathering of a community.*

Jesus knew himself to be the Messiah of God — that is, the Bearer of God's Redemptive Rule to men. True, not till the very end of his Ministry did he openly acknowledge his claim to the title (Mark xiv. 61 f.). Nevertheless, his whole Ministry — his words and deeds from the Baptism and the Temptation down to the Triumphal Entry and the Trial — are only fully intelligible if he knew that he was the Messiah. It is possible, of course, by performing some drastic critical surgery on the Gospels, to deny this. But such a view has never been accepted by the mass of sane and reasonable scholars.

The evidence of the Gospels shows that Jesus interpreted his vocation as Messiah in terms of two famous figures in the scriptures of his people — Isaiah's Servant of Jehovah and Daniel's " Son of man." The great " Ransom "-saying (Mark x. 45), with its allusions on the one hand to the " Son of man " and on the other to the idea of " serving " and the " giving of life " for " *the many,*" shows the fusion of these two Old Testament figures in Jesus' conception of his Messianic destiny.

Now, it is of capital importance to observe that both these Old Testament figures are *societary* figures. Each of them implies a community. As you cannot think of a shepherd without thinking also of his flock, so you cannot think of the Servant of Jehovah in Second Isaiah or of that mysterious " one like unto a son of man " in the seventh chapter of Daniel, without also thinking of Israel or " the people of the saints of the Most High."

Of the Isaianic Servant it has been truly written: " An inner relationship between the Messiah and the community first occurs in Second Isaiah. The 'Servant' becomes through his expiatory suffering the creator of the new people of God. So close is the connexion that we must speak of 'an inclusive relationship' between the Saviour-servant and the saved community. The existence of the Saviour and the People of God are bound up with each other." [10]

But Jesus also thought of himself in terms of "the son of man." Dead seas of critical ink have gone to the discussion of this enigmatic title; but scholars agree, on the whole, that it goes back *ultimately* to Dan. vii. 13. [11] Now, in that chapter there are two "moments" (although scholars for long neglected the second one): first, there appears (verse 13) a mysterious someone "like unto a son of man"; later (in the interpretation, verses 17 ff.) Daniel learns that this someone *represents* "the saints of the Most High."

Jesus had read that chapter (cf. *e.g.*, Mark xiv. 62). But how did he read it? Clearly Jesus regarded himself as that "someone" who was destined to "receive dominion and glory and a kingdom." That "someone" was the Messiah, *i.e.* himself. But Jesus surely read, and understood, the *whole* chapter. He must therefore have regarded himself as the *representative,* or head, of a special people, the saints of the Most High. His task then, as the Bearer of God's Rule, was to create this People; and for him his disciple-band was its nucleus.

This is the view of the German scholar Kattenbusch, [12] who boldly describes Daniel vii. as "the source of the Church-idea."

If this brief argument has any cogency, we are entitled to say that Jesus' conception of Messiahship necessitated the gathering of a community — call it what you will, the Remnant of the Last Days, the New People of God, the Church.

(3) The third argument (really a corollary of the sec-

ond), may be put thus: *The Shepherd must needs have a flock: when Jesus speaks of himself as doing a shepherd's work and of his disciples as a flock, he is describing his Messianic task of gathering the People of God.*

Everyone who has sung the metrical hundredth Psalm with its lines:

> " We are His flock He doth us feed,
> And for His sheep He doth us take,"

knows that " His flock " is the Psalmist's picturesque phrase for the People of God. But not quite everyone knows that in the prophets God, or his Messiah,[13] is commonly called the Shepherd and the community of the faithful, especially the community that shall survive the Divine Judgment on Israel, *i.e.* the Remnant, is called " His flock." The gathering of such a community is prophesied in Ezekiel xxxiv:

" As a shepherd seeketh out his flock in the day that he is among his sheep that are scattered abroad, so will I seek out my sheep; and I will deliver them out of all places whither they have been scattered in the cloudy and dark day. . . . I will seek that which was lost . . . and I will set up one shepherd over them, and he shall feed them, even my servant David " (Ezek. xxxiv. 12, 16, 23).

And in the famous prophecy of Micah it is prophesied of the coming Messiah, the One " who shall be our peace ":

" And he shall stand, and shall feed his flock in the strength of the Lord " (Mic. v. 4).

Further passages might be added in proof of this belief, this eschatological hope that in " the last days " when God's salvation should be manifested, Messiah's task should be to gather and tend God's flock.

Now this is what Jesus in the Gospels does, and how he speaks. His concern is with a " flock "; his mission to gather " lost sheep."

Consider the Parable of the Lost Sheep (Luke xv. 3–6; Matt. xviii. 12–13). Nowadays we generally think of the parable in relation to Jesus' new doctrine of God — the God who goes out actively to seek his lost children. But if we enquire after its " life-setting " in the Ministry of Jesus, it seems likely that the parable was originally an *ad hoc* reply of Jesus to certain critics who complained of his friendliness with " publicans and sinners." The subject of the parable is Jesus himself — he is the Shepherd; and he describes his mission as a quest for the lost sheep of God. Similarly, in Luke xix. 10 he says, " The Son of Man came to *seek* and to save *that which was lost.*" The rôle of the Son of Man is that of a Shepherd — the Shepherd, indeed, of Ezekiel xxxiv, 16: " I will seek that which was lost."

Furthermore, Jesus speaks not once but several times of his " flock ":

When he sends the disciples out on their mission, it is with the words: " Behold I send you forth as *sheep* . . ." (Matt. x. 16). On another occasion he thus addresses them: " Fear not, *little flock,* for it is your Father's good pleasure to give you the Kingdom " (Luke xii. 32).

And when the end is nigh, he borrows some words from Zechariah: " I will smite the Shepherd and the *sheep* shall be scattered abroad." Not only so, but in the next verse, speaking of his Resurrection, it is a *pastoral* verb which he employs: " I will *go before you* (προάξω ὑμᾶς) into Galilee " (Mark xiv. 27–28).

Though we may not quote the Fourth Gospel with the same confidence as a source for the actual words of Jesus, its testimony as a record of Jesus' Message and Mission, seen through the Christian experience of two generations, is not to be lightly set aside.

"I am the good shepherd," says Jesus in the Fourth Gospel, "and I know mine own . . . and I lay down my life for the sheep" (John x. 14 f.). The purpose of the Shepherd's dying is that he may "*gather* into one the children of God that are *scattered* abroad" (John xi. 52). With singular fitness therefore the charge of the Risen Lord to Peter expresses itself in the pastoral words: "Feed my sheep" (John xxi. 17). And it is but the echo of this great conception "spoken through" the old prophets and incarnated in Jesus and "his own," that we hear in the writings of the apostolic men. "For ye were going astray like sheep; but are now returned to the Shepherd and Bishop of your souls" (1 Pet. ii. 25): "The God of peace who brought again from the dead the *great shepherd of the sheep* with the blood of the eternal covenant, even our Lord Jesus" (Heb. xiii. 20).

(4) In a sense all our previous arguments have been *prolegomena* to the fourth. We have argued that everything in Jesus' preaching and teaching — his gospel of God's "redemptive Rule in action," his conception of his Messiahship, his words about the Shepherd and his Flock — demand, in spiritual logic, the creation of a people of God, a community. Now we must study Jesus as he does the thing itself, translates the idea into fact, clothes the conception with reality.

Therefore the fourth argument is as follows: That *Jesus called twelve disciples, that he taught them, that he sent them forth on a mission, that he instituted a covenant with them — all these facts show Jesus deliberately executing his Messianic task of creating a new Israel, the true people of God.*

Jesus *called* twelve disciples. To see that action in its true spiritual perspective we must turn back to a passage in Isaiah: " Bind thou up the testimony, seal the law among my disciples. And I will wait for the Lord, that hideth his face from the house of Jacob, and I will look for him. Behold, I and the children whom the Lord hath given me are for signs and wonders in Israel from the Lord of hosts, which dwelleth in Mount Zion " (Isa. viii. 16–18). At a certain stage in his career Isaiah gathered disciples around him and committed to them a record of his teaching. These disciples, " the children whom the Lord had given him," were, in fact, the realization of Isaiah's doctrine of the Remnant. " By this solemn act," says Skinner,[14] " Isaiah forms an inner circle of religious fellowship which is the nucleus of the new people of God." Robertson Smith says even more boldly: " The formation of this little community was a new thing in the history of religion. It was the birth of a new era in Old Testament religion; for it was the birth of the conception of the Church."[15] In the light of that passage (with the two comments) Jesus' action declared at the outset of his ministry that he purposed to create a new People of God. No less significant is the number called to close fellowship with himself. " He appointed *twelve* . . ." (Mark iii. 14). It is the number of the tribes of Israel. As soon as he remarked that number, every Jew of any spiritual penetration must have scented " a Messianic programme." By his choice of twelve disciples Jesus signified his intention to create a new Israel, a new *ecclesia,* a new Church.[16]

But Jesus not only called disciples; he also *taught* them. That teaching has been conveniently collected by the first Evangelist in what we know as " The Sermon on the Mount " (Matt. v.–vii.). To call it (as one scholar has done) " an ordination sermon for the Twelve " is to suggest that the Sermon was all delivered on one occasion, which it was not, and that it was restricted to the Twelve, which it probably was not. Nevertheless the Sermon is essentially *disciple-teaching,* instruction addressed not to the multitudes but to an inner circle of religious fellowship. It is, in fact, teaching for " the men of the Kingdom," for those who by repentance and faith have accepted " the Redemptive Rule of God " now being manifested in Jesus. The contents of the Sermon — sayings like those in which the hearers are called " the salt of the earth " and " the light of the world," the instructions about the practice of true religion, including the disciples' prayer, in vi. 1–18, the Golden Rule, etc. — all suggest instruction for a special community. The German scholar Windisch makes the point in a sentence: " These sayings of the Sermon on the Mount pave the way for a *secessio,* the formation of a new community." [17]

But Jesus not only called and taught disciples; he *" sent them forth "* as his commissioned and empowered envoys (that is the root meaning of " apostle ") on a special mission (Mark vi. 7–13, 30; Matt. x. 1–40; Luke ix. 1–6, x. 1–20. The mission of the Seventy is probably a " doublet " of the mission of the Twelve).

That mission, since it has left traces in all four Gospel sources, must rank as one of the best attested facts in the life of Jesus. It is a great pity that we do not know more about it. (If only Peter or John had kept a travel-diary and it had come down to us!) What we do know may be briefly summarized thus: Jesus sent his envoys out two by two, and before they left, gave them their " marching orders ": they were to travel with the barest equipment, and their task was to be the proclamation of the Redemptive Rule of God both by word and deed (*i.e.* by preaching and healing) in the towns and cities. Some would accept their message and entertain them; others would reject them (these were to be solemnly warned). And throughout their mission they were to remember whose ambassadors they were: " he who receives you receives me; and he who receives me receives him that sent me " (Matt. x. 40; cf. Luke x. 16). Then the veil is drawn over their activities (save for one incident during the mission — the case of the strange exorcist, Mark ix. 38 ff.[18]) and we hear no more until the " envoys " return and report to Jesus.

What was the specific purpose of this mission? A study of the Mission Charge will help us to an answer. The " envoys " were to preach the Redemptive Rule of God as a present and creative reality: " the Rule of God has come upon you " (Luke x. 9). But the Rule of God is, as we have seen, dynamic. It *creates* a people ruled, wherever its power is felt. Therefore the " envoys " of Jesus who brought God's Redemptive Rule to men must have " made converts," must have gathered believers. If some rejected their message, others accepted it and numbered themselves with the " little flock " of Jesus. And he who received the envoys, received their Sender; received not only the Sender, but also the redeeming God whose Rule gathers men into a community. The conclusion therefore is fairly clear, that the purpose of the mission was *the gathering of God's people.* There is sufficient evidence in the Gospels to show that the mission achieved its purpose (Mark vi. 30; Luke x. 17 ff.).

Finally, we must consider the Last Supper. " And he took a cup, and when he had given thanks, he gave to them and they all drank of it. And he said to them, This is my blood of the covenant which is shed for many " (Mark xiv. 23 f.). Paul's version of the word is, " This cup is the new covenant in my blood " (1 Cor. xi. 25). Jesus declared that by his death he was establishing a covenant — a

" new " covenant, as Paul's version has it. Now, the establishment of a covenant implies a community, a people of
God. The establishment of a new covenant must imply
the existence of a new people of God. Indeed, Jesus' words
(in Paul's version which has a good claim to be considered
original [19]) echo the great prophecy of the New Covenant
in Jeremiah xxxi. with its explicit promise: " I will be their
God and they shall be my people." The point of this is
fairly obvious. Hort saw it long ago: " The twelve," he
wrote, " sat that evening as representatives of the *ecclesia*
at large." [20]

Our arguments, now at an end, have tried to show that
Jesus during his Ministry gave himself to the high purpose
of creating a new people of God. But that purpose, he fore-
saw, could only be consummated by the death of himself,
the Servant-Messiah, who came to give his life a ransom for
many. There is a saying of Jesus, whose precise words may
be hard to reconstruct but whose substantial authenticity
it is difficult to question. According to John, it ran: " Destroy this temple and in three days I will raise it up " (John
ii. 19). According to Jesus' accusers in Mark xiv. 58, it ran:
" I will destroy this temple made with hands and in three
days build another made without hands." Modern scholars [21] are almost unanimous in finding here an *ecclesia*-
saying. What underlies these two versions is not so much
a direct prophecy of the Resurrection, a *Resurgam,* as a
prophecy of a new Church. Jesus looks forward to a time
beyond his death when there will be a new shrine " made
without hands " for the worship of his " little flock " who
are the first-fruits of the new people of God.

The fulfilment of that prophecy in the Apostolic Church
forms the subject of our next chapter.

NOTES

1 So Hatch, *The Origin of the Early Christian Churches*, 1881.

2 *E.g.* in Jackson and Lake, *The Beginnings of Christianity*, Vol. I, p. 317: "Jesus in the earliest tradition of the Synoptic Gospels does not appear as intending to found a new society." The dogma dies hard.

3 *Malku;* Heb. *malkuth*.

4 Cf. Bultmann, *Jesus*, p. 140: "We cannot speak of God as Jesus did unless we speak of his *action*."

5 *The Kingdom of God and the Son of Man*, pp. 108–112.

6 H. E. Weber quoted by Gloege, *Reich Gottes und Kirche*, p. 202 (note).

7 In both passages Moffatt translates " Realm."

8 See Flew, *Jesus and His Church*, pp. 36–39.

9 T. W. Manson, *The Teaching of Jesus*, p. 206: "In the mind of Jesus to become a genuine disciple of his and to enter into the Kingdom amounted to much the same thing."

10 Gloege, *Reich Gottes und Kirche*, pp. 217 f.

11 H. R. Mackintosh, *The Person of Jesus Christ*, p. 21: "One of the few points on which scholars have reached virtual agreement."

12 See his essay, " Der Quellort der Kirchenidee " in *Festgabe für A. von Harnack*.

13 Jeremias, *Jesus als Weltvollender*, pp. 32 f.: "Shepherd was a common name in the East to describe the bringer of Salvation."

14 *Isaiah* (Camb. Bible), p. 70.

15 *The Prophets of Israel*, pp. 274–5.

16 The choice of Matthias to replace Judas (Acts i. 15 ff.) shows that the apostles understood the significance of the number twelve.

17 *Der Sinn der Bergpredigt*, p. 46.

18 This is surely the *Sitz im Leben* of this " Pronouncement Story." It clearly belongs to a time when the Twelve were separated from Jesus.

19 So Behm and Flew.

20 *Christian Ecclesia*, p. 30.

21 See W. Manson, *The Incarnate Glory*, pp. 83–6; Flew, *Jesus and his Church*, pp. 55–8; Otto, *The Kingdom of God and the Son of Man*, p. 62. Cf. *The Epistle of Barnabas*, xvi. The writer, apparently echoing Mk. xiv. 58, states that the " spiritual temple " then being built up is the company of Christian believers.

CHAPTER SEVEN

THE APOSTLES AND THE CHURCH

THE DEATH OF "the Shepherd" which at first scattered "the little flock" and seemed to write *finis* to its history, proved, by the mercy of God, to be not an end but only a beginning.[1] With the Resurrection and Pentecost the little community began a new and glorious chapter in its history.

The story of the Primitive Church is told in the early chapters of Acts. It is a story which, though very fragmentary, seems in the main trustworthy; and from these chapters we gain a broad impression of what the earliest believers thought about themselves. While we ought not, perhaps, to speak of them as having "a doctrine of the Church," they certainly held certain *basic convictions* about themselves. Thus, they believed (1) that they were the true people of God who had served themselves heirs to the promises forfeited by "Israel after the flesh"; (2) that the bond of their union was a common allegiance to *Maran*-Jesus; (3) that, as the prophets (*e.g.* Joel ii. 28 f.; Ezek. xxxvi. 26 f.) had predicted, they had been signally endowed with God's Spirit; and (4) that they had a message to deliver (*i.e.* the *kerygma* already discussed) and a mission to fulfil.

These four convictions had their roots in the historic ministry of Jesus. As we have seen, Jesus had conceived of his little band as the true Israel; he had called again and again for personal attachment to himself; he had promised that his disciples should receive divine power;[2] and he had sent forth his disciples on at least one mission.

These four convictions reappear, *mutatis mutandis,* in all subsequent apostolic thinking about the Church — as we propose to show.

So let us turn to the records of the earliest Church preserved in Acts, and examine the evidence for these four " basic convictions " of which we have spoken.

(1) THE PRIMITIVE CHURCH

(A) The People of God

In the early chapters of Acts we find the little company of believers in Jesus the Messiah called "The *Ecclesia*" (*e.g.* v. 11, viii. 1, 3). The word itself, *ecclesia,* was familiar enough to those who spoke the *Koinē*. For the Greek of those days it signified *a popular assembly;* and indeed occurs in that sense thrice in the nineteenth chapter of Acts (verses 32, 39, and 41). But it is certain that a Greek of those days hearing the Christians style themselves " the *ecclesia*" — and especially " the *ecclesia* of God "[3] — would have been puzzled at the use of the article and the obviously peculiar connotation of the word. But if that Greek had become " a God-fearer " and taken to reading the Greek Old Testament, his mystification would have vanished; for the source of the Christians' strange self-designation was the Septuagint. There, as a rule, *ecclesia* translates *Qahal* (ἐκκλησία κυρίου = Q^{e}hal Yahweh), and *Qahal* in the Hebrew Old Testament is the usual term for Israel as the gathered people of God. The use of *ecclesia* in those early chapters of Acts has nothing to do with Greek guilds or the like. The Christians' choice of that word expressed their claim to be the true people of God at once old and new.

Of course, it is chiefly the Christian community in *Jerusalem* that is called " the *ecclesia*" in those early chapters of Acts. But the *local* connexion is not the primary thing; for in ix. 31 we read of " the *ecclesia* throughout all Judæa and Galilee and Samaria." Originally, therefore, the *ecclesia* was domiciled in Jerusalem; but when little groups of Christians arose elsewhere, there developed the idea of the local *ecclesia* as a microcosm (or embodiment) of the one *ecclesia*; they — these local communities — were severally " churches" as belonging to the one " Church."

The claim to be the true people of God is implied in the term " the *ecclesia*"; but it also appears in passages from the primitive *kerygma* where the term itself is not found, *e.g.* Acts iii. 25–26, which reflects the proud claim of the earliest Christians to be not a party within Israel but Israel itself, the people of God, to whom in Jesus belong the promises made to God's chosen people.

(B) The Allegiance of the " Ecclesia "

Since we have already dealt with this subject in our section on the Christology of the Primitive Church, we need not dwell on it now. The focal point of the earliest *ecclesia's* spiritual life was their devotion to *Maran*-Jesus. He was their exalted Messiah and Lord. " In his name " they baptized converts (Acts ii. 38, viii. 16); " in his name " they healed the sick (Acts iii. 6); to him they addressed prayer (Acts vii. 59); and " Jesus is Lord " was probably the earliest Christian creed.[4]

(C) The Community of the Spirit

The earliest Christians knew themselves as the community of the Spirit. Whatever we think about Acts ii., and especially the references to the " tongues as of fire " and the polyglot endowment of the disciples, only the very sceptical would deny the basic fact which Luke's narrative aims to record — that on a definite occasion the little group of Christians in Jerusalem experienced an extraordinary access of new power which they identified with the Spirit of God mediated by the exalted Christ, and which they interpreted as the fulfilment of Old Testament prophecy. This Spirit which moved among the little company of God's people manifested itself in various ways — in ecstatic speech (ii. 4), in the power to heal sickness, in the " rapture " of Philip (viii. 39), in the eloquence of Stephen; and so on. The concomitants of the Spirit were " power," " glad fearlessness " (iv. 31, παρρησία) and " faith " (vi. 5). All this is the language not of systematic theology but of experimental religion; we are dealing with men who have experienced (to borrow Anderson Scott's phrase) [5] " the uprush of life," who have had a new and vitalizing experience of God's activity in the present, who know themselves empowered by God to deliver a message and fulfil a mission.

(D) The Mission of the " Ecclesia "

As the People of God, " the Saved and Saving Remnant," the Christian *ecclesia* must have been conscious of a mission from the beginning. Perhaps at first they took " short views " — did they not expect an imminent end of the world? — and construed the primary purpose of their mission as the conversion of their unbelieving fellow-Jews. " To you is the promise and to your children," says Peter to the " men of Judæa " (Acts ii. 39); but he proceeds, significantly, " and to all that are afar off, even as many as the Lord our God shall call unto him," where we need not restrict the reference to the Jews of the Dispersion (cf. Eph. ii. 13 and 17). Of a similar import is the quotation, in Acts iii. 25, of the promise made of old to Abraham, " and in thy seed shall all the families of the earth be blessed " (cf. Gal. iii. 8).[6] In such passages, if we may regard them as preserving the outlook of the earliest days, we may perceive wider horizons rising up before the Primitive Church. In the speech of the Hellenist Stephen (Acts vii.) (which even the editors of the *Beginnings of Christianity* admit may preserve the gist of what Stephen said) the vision of a wider mission emerges; for Stephen taught the supersession of the Temple cultus, and the corollary of that proposition is that the People of God is not " thirled " to any one place. It was given to one Paul of Tarsus to grasp the fullest implications of the Proto-martyr's conviction.

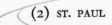

(2) ST. PAUL

St. Paul undoubtedly enriched and developed the early Christian conception of the Church. This is specially clear in his later epistles, Colossians and Ephesians; but his basic conception of it is not different from that of the earliest Christians.

(A) The " Ecclesia " or People of God

Though Paul writes for the most part to Gentiles and though he does not always see eye to eye with the leaders of the Mother Church, he speaks of the *ecclesia* essentially as they did.

This is not at first sight obvious, for Paul's language about the *ecclesia* is very varied. Sometimes for him it is simply " the *ecclesia* " (as in the nine examples in Ephesians); sometimes it is " the *ecclesiæ* " (there are half a dozen instances in 2 Corinthians). Often he adds the words " of God " (both to singular and plural). Sometimes by *ecclesia* he means the whole number of Christians; often the local community (the place-name, " Cenchreæ " or " Galatia " being inserted); and four times a house-church. Yet always the *inclusive* " people-of-God " sense remains primary for St. Paul; and the local sense is second-ary. (An admirable discussion is to be found in K. L. Schmidt's article *ecclesia* in Kittel's new *Theological Vocabulary*. All we can do here is to notice some of the more striking evidence.)

As Schmidt puts it,[7] " Not an addition of single com-munities gives the *ecclesia*. Every community, however small, represents the whole Church." Thus, in 1 Cor. i. 2 (as also in 2 Cor. i. 1) $\tau\hat{\eta}$ $\dot{\epsilon}\kappa\kappa\lambda\eta\sigma\dot{\iota}\alpha$ . . . $\tau\hat{\eta}$ $o\check{v}\sigma\eta$ $\dot{\epsilon}\nu$ $Ko\rho\dot{\iota}\nu\theta\omega$ is *not* to be rendered " the Corinthian Church " (beside which we might set, say, " the Roman Church "), but " the Church (of God) as it is in Corinth." " The mystery which is ' Israel ' is present in Corinth, having its local embodiment in the Christian community there, as it simi-larly has in other places where there are those who call on His name."[8] Likewise, the inclusive sense is very clear in 1 Cor. x. 32, " Give no offence to Jews and Greeks and to the *ecclesia* of God," where the idea of Christians as " a third race " is unmistakable. Other good examples are: 1 Cor. xii. 28, xv. 9; Gal. i. 13; Phil. iii. 6; Col. i. 24; and all the examples in Ephesians.

Moreover, there are many passages where the thing without the word is found. Such are " the Israel of God " (Gal. vi. 16), or " we are the circumcision " (Phil. iii. 3) where " the thought (as Dibelius says[9]) is not of the bodily mark but of the community's conviction that they are the new People of God " (cf. Rom. ix. 24, 27).

(B) The Allegiance of the " Ecclesia "

For Paul, as for the Jerusalem Church, the *ecclesia* is constituted by its allegiance to Jesus as Lord. " If thou shalt confess Jesus as Lord . . . thou shalt be saved "

(Rom. x. 9). " No man," Paul declares, " can say: ' Jesus is Lord,' but in the Holy Spirit " (1 Cor. xii. 3; cf. Phil. ii. 9–11). But it is in Paul's phrase " in Christ " that the common allegiance of the *ecclesia* to Christ finds its most remarkable expression. No doubt " being in Christ " often describes (as Deissmann said) the individual Christian's intensely intimate fellowship with the living Christ. But some more adequate explanation is demanded by passages like " of Him (*i.e.* God) are ye in Christ Jesus " (1 Cor. i. 30); " There is therefore now no condemnation to them that are in Christ Jesus" (Rom. viii. 1); " the saints and faithful brethren in Christ at Colossæ " (Col. i. 2), etc. The clue is to be found in the Hebrew concept of corporate personality: in passages like these Paul conceives of Christ as *the Inclusive Representative of a new humanity;* so that " to be in Christ " is to be one of the New People of God of which Christ is the Head. Nothing could better show how closely their allegiance to Christ binds believers into the sacred society, which is the Church.

(C) The Community of the Spirit

For Paul, as for the Primitive Church in Jerusalem, the *ecclesia* was the community of the Spirit.

St. Paul's conception of the Spirit is not really different from that of the earliest believers.[10] All that we can discover is a change of emphasis. Whereas the earliest Christians were prone to find the most notable manifestations of the Spirit in certain psycho-physical phenomena like *glossolalia,* Paul sought to win his converts — especially in Corinth — to worthier ways of regarding it — to see the Spirit as the dynamic of all victorious Christian living and to find its finest fruits in love and joy and peace; in short, to regard the Spirit as the cause " not only of religious experiences but of religious experience."

But that the Spirit was the power by which the *ecclesia* lived and the source of its "togetherness," [11] Paul was as sure as the men of Jerusalem. The Church, he says, is a temple filled by God's Spirit (Eph. ii. 21 f.; 1 Cor. iii. 16); and in two famous passages he calls it "the Fellowship of the Spirit"; "if then there is any consolation in Christ," he writes to the Philippians (ii. 1), "any comfort of love, if *the Spirit has really created a fellowship* . . ."; and at the close of the Second Epistle to the Corinthians (xiii. 14) he prays that "the fellowship created by the Spirit" (not "the companionship of the Spirit") may continue among them.

(D) The Mission of the "Ecclesia"

If James and his friends had any misgivings about the universal nature of the Church's mission before the Apostolic Council, Paul had none. In what is possibly his earliest letter, he describes the limits of the *ecclesia* — and sets no limit to them: "There can be neither Jew nor Greek, there can be neither bond nor free, there can be no male and female; for ye are all one man in Christ Jesus " (Gal. iii. 28). In one of his last letters he defines the mission of the *ecclesia* as the reconciliation of all things to God through Christ (Col. i. 20). And while always there lurked in his mind the idea that the Jews had "some advantage" [12] (Rom. iii. 1) and that salvation was for "the Jew first " (Rom. i. 16) he saw more clearly than any other of the apostles the full import of that *testimonium* which seems to have figured prominently in the Apostolic preaching: "In thy seed shall all the families of the earth be blessed " (Gal. iii. 8 = Acts iii. 25).

(3) FIRST PETER

(A) The People of God

If the word *ecclesia* nowhere occurs, the idea bulks large in 1 Peter. The opening description of the readers (i. 1) proclaims them the true Israel scattered in an alien world; and title after title originally applied to God's ancient people is now bestowed on the Asiatic Christian communities who (to judge from the epistle) were predominantly Gentile: they are "the flock of God" (v. 2 f.), God's house (iv. 17), the elect race, a royal priesthood, a people for God's own possession, who in time past were no people but are now the people of God (ii. 9–10).

(B) The Allegiance of the "Ecclesia"

Two passages are specially relevant. In one (iii. 15) Peter urges his readers "to consecrate the Christ as Lord in their hearts." In the other (ii. 4 f.) he likens the Church to a spiritual house built around Christ as the corner-stone — so close-knit is the unity of Christians in their common allegiance to their Lord.

(C) The Community of the Spirit

There is an opening allusion to the "hallowing" of the true Israel "by the Spirit" (i. 2); but it is in ii. 5 that Peter most clearly characterizes the Church as the home of the Spirit: it is, he says, an οἶκος πνευματικός — a house whose cement, so to speak, is the indwelling Spirit of God, a house whose "living stones" are called on to offer up "spiritual sacrifices," *i.e.* acts of self-oblation inspired by the Spirit (cf. also iv. 14).

(D) The Mission of the " Ecclesia "

Little is said of this. The Church's mission is to pro-
mote God's glory (iv. 11). Christian wives are told how
they may " gain " unbelieving husbands for the Faith (iii.
1), as Christians generally are advised that worthy behav-
iour among the Gentiles may not only silence their slanders
but lead them to " glorify God in the day of visitation " (ii.
12).

(4) HEBREWS

(A) The Church as the People of God

The actual word *ecclesia* occurs but twice in Hebrews:
ii. 12 and xii. 23. The latter instance, since it refers to the
Heavenly Jerusalem, does not concern us. In the first passage, a quotation from Psalm xxii. is set on Jesus' lips:

> I will declare thy name unto my brethren,
> In the midst of the *ecclesia* (*Qahal*) will I sing thy praise,

and is followed by two quotations, the first from Isa. viii. 17,
and the second from Isa. viii. 18: " Behold I and the children which God hath given me " (a reference, in the original, to Isaiah and his disciples). This deft use of the Old
Testament suggests the author's conception of the Christian Church: the company of God's people gathered about
Jesus the Son of God.

But if the word *ecclesia* is rare, the conception of the
Church as the true people of God pervades the epistle.
Thus, " so then there remaineth a sabbath rest for the people of God " (iv. 9) — a rest which God's ancient people
had refused and which is now offered anew to Christians.
Or " I will be their God and they shall be my people " (viii.
10), where Jeremiah's prophecy of the New Covenant is
applied to the Christian Church. Or, " wherefore Jesus

also, that he might sanctify the people through his own blood, suffered without the gate " (xiii. 12). And in truth, particular texts apart, there runs through the epistle the conviction that the Christian *ecclesia* is the true heir of the promises forfeited by the ancient people of God.

(B) Allegiance to Christ

" Consider," said the author, " the Envoy and High Priest of our *confession,* even Jesus " (iii. 1; cf. iv. 14). This Jesus whom they " confess " is Founder of the household of God (iii. 3) and as " Son " is set over it (iii. 6); and this household is the Christian Church: " we are this household " (iii. 6). So, using his own idioms and figures, the writer to the Hebrews suggests the allegiance of the *ecclesia* to Christ.

(C) The Community of the Spirit

The doctrine of the Spirit is not prominent in Hebrews; but there are sufficient references to show that the writer held the same view of the Spirit's activity in the Church which we have found elsewhere. When first they received the Gospel, God had authenticated the message of the preachers " both by signs and wonders and by manifold powers and by gifts of the Holy Spirit " (ii. 4); they had been " made partakers of the Holy Spirit " and had " tasted the good word of God and the powers of the Age to come " (vi. 4 f.). Woe betide those therefore at the Judgment who have " trodden under foot the Son of God " and " done despite to the Spirit of grace " (x. 29).

(D) The Mission of the " Ecclesia "

Since the writer's aim is to warn his readers against the danger of apostasy from the living God (and not to provide us with a doctrine of the Church) little is expressly

said about the mission of the Church.[13]   But the universal
mission of the *ecclesia* is the necessary corollary of the writer's main proposition — that Christianity is the final and
absolute religion.   Such a religion must be meant for all
mankind.

(5) ST. JOHN AND THE " ECCLESIA "

(A) The People of God

Neither the Gospel nor the First Epistle of John contains
the word *ecclesia*.   But in the allegories of the Shepherd
and his Flock (John x. 1–16) and of the Vine and the
Branches (John xv. 1 ff.), we have the Johannine doctrine
of the Church as the true people of God.   John x. 11 ff.
(" I am the good Shepherd," etc.) reads like a Johannine
meditation on Jesus' conception of himself and his disciples
as the little flock of God under its Shepherd the Messiah
(see previous chapter).   Even more illuminating is the al-
legory of the Vine, which is Christ, and the branches,
which are the disciples.   When we recall that the Vine is
a favourite Old Testament symbol for Israel not as a nation
but as the people of God [14] (see, *e.g.,* Psalm lxxx. 8 ff.; Jer.
ii. 21; Ezek. xv. 1 ff.   In the coins of the Maccabees Israel
is represented as a vine), Jesus' words, " I am the true (genuine) vine . . . ye are the branches," are seen to be a clear
claim that he and his disciples are the true Israel of God.
The adoption of the metaphor here to illustrate the mysti-
cal relation between Christ and his believing followers sig-
nifies the supersession of the ancient theocracy by the new
society of Jesus.[15]

(B) The Allegiance of the " Ecclesia "

In the Johannine writings the distinctive name for Jesus
is " Son " or " Son of God."   Therefore while Paul and

others sum up the allegiance of the *ecclesia* in the phrase
" Jesus is Lord," John prefers the confession " Jesus is the
Son of God " (1 John iv. 15, v. 5), and speaks of "believing in the name of his Son Jesus Christ" (1 John iii. 23,
etc.; John xi. 27, xx. 31). The *ecclesia's* close adhesion to
Jesus as its head finds expression in the words " Abide in
me " (the word " abide " occurs ten times in John xv. 4–10)
". . . apart from me ye can do nothing" (John xv. 4 f.).
Worthy of observation is John's finely ethical insistence
that true allegiance to Jesus involves the fulfilment of his
commands: " he that saith he abideth in him ought himself also to walk as he walked " (1 John ii. 6; cf. John xiv.
21).

(C) The Community of the Spirit

Like the rest of the apostolic writers, John thinks of
the *ecclesia* or people of God as a fellowship united by the
Holy Spirit.

John's general conception of the Spirit is substantially
the same as Paul's; but, whereas Paul regarded the Spirit
as the motive energy of the whole Christian life, John
specially conceives of the Paraclete as " the *enlightening*
Spirit " who after Christ's departure serves as his *alter ego*
and interprets the revelation made by Christ to his followers.

But in his teaching generally about the Spirit and the
Church, John agrees with our other witnesses. It is at
Baptism, the rite of initiation into the *ecclesia,* that the
Spirit is received (John iii. 5). The sphere of the Spirit's
operation is the *ecclesia* (xiv. 15 f.); and it is on the disciples
as the *ecclesia in nuce* [16] that the Spirit is bestowed by the
risen Jesus (xx. 22).[17] The members of the *ecclesia* are
assured that God abides in them by the gift of the Spirit —
the " chrism " — which they have received (1 John iii. 24,

iv. 13). And the Spirit bears witness to Christ (John xv. 26; 1 John v. 7); for he is "the Spirit of Truth," and his function is to guide Christians "into all the Truth" (*i.e.* all the truth about Christ and his Gospel) (John xvi. 13).

(D) The Mission of the "Ecclesia"

As emphatically as the Apostle to the Gentiles, John teaches not only that the *ecclesia* has a mission but that it is universal (cf. iv. 21-24). As a foreshadowing of the *ecclesia's* mission clearly enunciated in xvii. 18 and xx. 21, he shows us Jesus during his Ministry in contact not only with Samaritans but also with Greeks; and elsewhere the words which Jesus addresses to his little community describe the universal mission: "Other sheep I have which are not of this fold: them also I must bring . . . and they shall become one flock, one shepherd" (x. 16). "Neither for these only do I pray, but for them also that believe on me through their word" (xvii. 20). For Jesus died, as the evangelist commenting on the high priest's words says, "not for the nation only, but that he might also gather into one the children of God that are scattered abroad" (John xi. 52).

To conclude. Once again the unity of the New Testament appears in the doctrine of the *ecclesia*. It is the people of God with a continuous life which goes back through the history of Israel; but it is the people of God reconstituted by Jesus the Messiah, its Lord and Head, signally endowed with God's Spirit, and conscious of a saving mission "to the Jew first and also to the Greek."

Many practical comments might be made. We shall content ourselves with making two:

(1) Since the *ecclesia* is so integral to the Christianity of the New Testament, any latter-day Christianity which

belittles the doctrine of the Church stands condemned by apostolic standards. Dr. Visser 't Hooft has said that Protestantism steadily refuses to take the Church seriously. It is a salutary reminder: the New Testament knows nothing of unattached Christians, as " the Bible knows nothing of solitary religion." To be a Christian means, according to the New Testament, to be a member of the New People of God created and constituted by God's saving act in Christ.[18]

(2) The true doctrine of the Church in the New Testament has a very real bearing on the problem of Re-union. " So long as scholars (like Hatch, Harnack, etc.) thought that independent communities combined to form the Church in the first instance, reversion to their original independence seemed justifiable. If the view set forward above is correct, that the Church was one from the beginning and by nature cannot be otherwise, disunion is clearly contrary to God's will." [19]

NOTES

1 Cf. Acts i. 1: " All that Jesus *began* both to do and to teach."

2 Mark xiii. 11; Luke xii. 12; Matt. x. 20 (Q); (cf. Luke xi. 13; Matt. vii. 11); Luke xxiv. 49. I also regard the sayings in John xiv.–xvi., where Jesus promises the Spirit to his disciples after he is gone, as evidence that Jesus gave fuller teaching to his disciples about the Spirit than the meagre data of the Gospels suggest. See *The Doctrine of the Holy Spirit* (Headingley Lectures), Lecture 2, by V. Taylor.

3 Acts xx. 28. Though " of God " does not occur in the earlier references to the *ecclesia* in Acts, it is always to be *understood*.

4 See *Paul and his Predecessors,* pp. 31, 46, and 102 f.

5 *The Fellowship of the Spirit,* p. 46.

6 The quotation of this testimonium by " Peter " and Paul and the πρῶτον-principle (Acts iii. 26; Rom. i. 16) is, as Knowling remarks (Exp. Grk. Test. Acts, *ad loc.*), " a striking illustration of the unity of apostolic preaching."

7 *Op. cit.*

8 Hebert, *The Throne of David*, p. 230.

9 *H.B.N.T. ad loc.*

10 See *Paul and his Predecessors*, ch. x.

11 The "togetherness" of the Jerusalem Church finds expression in the frequent use of ἐπὶ τὸ αὐτό (three times in Acts ii.).

12 Cf. Dodd on Rom. iii. 1: "His Pharisaism — or shall we say, his patriotism? — was too deeply engrained for him to put right out of his mind the idea that somehow the divine covenant with mankind had a most favoured nation clause."

13 Much, however, is implied. Christ, we are told, "tasted death for every man," has "brought many sons to glory," "has become the author of salvation to all that obey him"; so that the universal mission of the *Ecclesia* is clearly implied.

14 Gloege, *Reich Gottes,* p. 231.

15 W. Manson, *The Incarnate Glory*, pp. 200 f. We should add that in *The Didache* (ix. 2) the Vine of David is apparently the Messiah, and that perhaps the wine of the Last Supper suggested the vine imagery in John xv.

16 So Westcott.

17 This seems to be the Johannine version of Pentecost (Acts ii.); but the two narratives are not necessarily inconsistent. See W. Temple, *Readings in St. John's Gospel*, Series ii, p. 242.

18 J. S. Whale, *Christian Doctrine*, p. 19: "True Christian experience is always *ecclesiastical experience*."

19 Lowther Clarke, *Divine Humanity*, p. 155.

soteriology

III. One Salvation

CHAPTER EIGHT

SIN AND SALVATION

THE SALVATION of which the *kerygma* tells centres in Christ, and implies an *ecclesia*. Thus far has our argument taken us. Now we must say something concerning the Salvation itself. Therefore in our last two chapters we pass from Christology and Ecclesiology to Soteriology.

Soteriology in the New Testament is a vast subject, and we cannot hope to treat all the issues which it raises. But in any discussion of soteriology two issues stand out: (1) the problem of sin and (2) the means of atonement. We propose to concentrate on these two, and to consider them from the viewpoint of the unity of the New Testament. The two " propositions of unity " which we seek to maintain are as follows:

(1) In their view of man's sinful condition before God our Lord and St. Paul are essentially at one.

(2) In their approach to the soteriological focus of the New Testament — the death of Christ — the New Testament writers show a profound unity.

(I) GOD, MAN, AND SIN IN JESUS' TEACHING AND ST. PAUL'S

The claim that in this matter of man's sinful condition before God, our Lord and his great Apostle share essentially the same view, may seem at first sight manifestly absurd.

Why? The chief reason is that most of us are still

haunted by the ghost of the old controversy, " Jesus or Paul? " We have been taught to contrast Jesus and Paul — even to choose between them. One does not need to be very old to recall articles, essays, books which busied themselves with this problem; the radical scholars pointing out the differences between Jesus and Paul, the conservatives seeking to minimize them and to emphasize the points of similarity. Out of that controversy was born an epigram which blandly (and anachronistically) proclaimed: " Jesus was a Pelagian; Paul an Augustinian." Presumably its meaning is that in Jesus' view everyone born into the world is morally clean, need not inevitably sin, and may by his good deeds accumulate merit with God; whereas Paul teaches that Adam's fall has involved the whole race in guilt and made it impossible for any man to live a sinless and perfect life. It is a false antithesis, as we shall see; but the epigram serves to remind us how scholars thought (and sometimes still think) about Jesus and Paul. Thus instructed, it is not surprising that the ordinary thoughtful Christian assumes a wide cleavage between Jesus and Paul on the subject of man's sinfulness; that he contrasts the simple and glad " religion of Jesus " with the gloomy theology of Paul, and in short, that he supposes Jesus to have held fairly optimistic views of man and his " salvability " in contrast with Paul's obviously sombre views.

Does the New Testament evidence justify this antithesis between the Lord and the Apostle to the Gentiles? If not, if we can show that it is false — a serious obstacle in the way of our quest for the essential unity of New Testament teaching will have been removed.

To grasp the problem aright, we must begin with an examination of the attitude of Jesus and Paul to the law. Paradoxical though it may sound, it is true to say here that Jesus and Paul are fundamentally at one.[1]

(A) The Law

For both Jesus and Paul the law (or *Torah*) is the revelation of God's will for man. Jesus time and time again assumes its validity and truth. When he is asked, for example, " What shall I do that I may inherit eternal life? " he answers, " Thou knowest *the commandments* " (Mark x. 17 ff.). When he is asked, " What is the chief commandment? " he points to Deuteronomy vi. 4 f. and Leviticus xix. 19 (Mark xii. 29–31). When the Sadducees put their stock poser to him about the resurrection, he refers them to " the book of Moses " (Mark xii. 26). And he declares in explicit words, " Think not that I came to destroy the law or the prophets: I came not to destroy but to fulfil " (Matt. v. 17).

Paul, too, declares the law to be the revelation of God's will. Though he says that since the coming of " faith " (Gal. iii. 23) the law as a system of salvation is finished and done with,[2] he asserts in most emphatic terms that the law is the expression of the Divine will for man: " Is the law sin? God forbid. . . . The law is holy and the commandment holy, and righteous, and good. . . . We know that the law is spiritual " (Rom. vii. 7–14). And he agrees that he who fulfils the law gains life (Rom. ii. 10, x. 5).

(B) Observe next that both Jesus and Paul lay the emphasis on the *moral* requirements of the law. It is to these, " Do not kill, Do not commit adultery, Do not steal, etc.," that Jesus directs " the Rich Young Ruler " (Mark x. 17 ff.). In Mark vii. 9–13 he plays off the Fifth Commandment against the Scribes and Pharisees who practise *Corban*. And he singles out judgment and mercy as " the weightier matters of the law " (Matt. xxiii. 23). Paul, too, emphasizes the ethical aspects of the law. When speaking of the law in the famous seventh chapter of Romans he finds it necessary to take a concrete example, he says: "Howbeit, I had not known sin, except through the law," and then proceeds, " for I had not known coveting except the law had said, *Thou shall not covet*" (Rom. vii. 7). It is the Tenth Commandment that springs to his mind — the only commandment that deals with inward impulse rather than overt act. No less significant is the fact that in Rom. ii. 14 f. he regards the Gentiles' " conscience " (the moral law within) as their equivalent for the Jewish law.

(C) Finally, let us notice that for both Jesus and Paul *the commandment of love is the core and kernel of the law*. After quoting " Thou shalt love the Lord thy God with all thy heart " and setting beside it " Thou shalt love thy neighbour as thyself," Jesus concludes, " There is none other commandment greater than these " (Mark xii. 29–31). Paul says very much the same: twice over in Rom. xii. 8–10 he pronounces love " the fulfilment " or " sum total " of the law: " For this, Thou shalt not commit adultery, Thou shalt not steal, Thou shalt not covet, and if there be any other commandment, it is summed up in this word, namely, Thou shalt love thy neighbour as thyself. Love worketh no ill to his neighbour: love therefore is the fulfilment of the law " (cf. Gal. v. 14). Thus far, then, Jesus and Paul agree.

But Paul says that the law drives men to sin: " the strength of sin is the law " (1 Cor. xv. 56); " Through the law cometh the knowledge of sin " (Rom. iii. 20); " I had not known sin except through the law " (Rom. vii. 7). Not works of law, he declares, but God's grace alone can save men (Gal. ii. 16, etc.). Yet Paul does not mean that works of law are not God's will. (Had we so put it to him, he would have uttered a fervent " God forbid " and referred us to Rom. vii. 7–14.) Paul means that any attempt to *earn* salvation, to establish a claim as of right on God by a *tour de force* of law-works, is not only foredoomed to failure (he wrote out of his own bitter experience) but is presumptuous sin against God — the sin *par excellence* of the Jews who strove to establish their own righteousness and find " a matter for boasting," before God (Rom. x. 3 f.; Phil. iii. 9, etc.).

Jesus, of course, does not speak in this way; he does not theologize — or rabbinize — about sin as Paul does. Yet, if his language is very different, his fundamental view is the same. The slave who has done the things commanded has no " cause for boasting." Even so, says Jesus, when we have done all the things that are commanded we must own ourselves unworthy (*i.e.* not claiming merit) servants (Luke xvii. 7–10). What a startling parable it is! Most modern employers would be quite satisfied with *this minimum* — " all the things commanded " — from their employees! But God's requirement is incomparably more radical than man's. All our imagined righteousness is as filthy rags in his sight. " By works of law shall no man be justified."

" Is it enough to forgive an offending brother seven times? " Peter asks his Master hopefully. " Seven times! " says Jesus (in effect). " Nay, seventy times seven! There is *no enough* with God " (Matt. xviii. 21 f.). And Jesus no less than Paul knows that for the legalist in religion God's sheer grace to undeserving men must ever be a stumbling-block (Matt. xx. 14 f.).[3] Indeed the Sermon on the Mount[4] is not a new and more exacting law (else were Jesus laying on his disciples a heavier burden than ever the Scribes did) but a *reductio ad absurdum* of legalism.[5] For in the great antitheses of Matt. v. 21–48 Jesus makes plain the contrast between the law interpreted as a code of regulations by the performance of which a man may found a claim on God's favour, and God's will with its utterly radical requirements of righteousness.

But we can carry the parallel between Jesus' teaching and Paul's a good deal farther:

(II) JUSTIFICATION BY FAITH IN JESUS' TEACHING AND ST. PAUL'S

We commonly suppose "justification by faith and not by works" to be Paul's peculiar conception of Christian salvation: if a man would "get right with God," he must renounce the vain attempt to establish his own righteousness before God, and owning his own unrighteousness cast himself on God's free grace and forgiveness in Jesus Christ. If we study words only this supposition appears to be entirely warranted; for we find the word "justified" but once on Jesus' lips in the Gospels (Luke xviii. 14) and Paul's antithesis of faith and works never. But how mistaken is the supposition, appears when we examine the content of Jesus' teaching, for there the thing itself, if not the words, is indubitably present.

Consider the Parable of the Prodigal Son (Luke xv. 11–32). It teaches exactly what St. Paul means by justification: its message can be put in a phrase of St. Paul: " God who justifies the ungodly" (Rom. iv. 5). If we ask first, What does the parable teach about God? the answer is, God is a *God of sheer grace*. The point, however, needs a word or two of explanation. According to Jülicher, Jesus' parables using simple analogies from life compelled his hearers to admit as "self-evident" similar truth in the spiritual realm; and Jülicher quotes the Parable of the Prodigal Son as a clear case in point. The hearer has to own that it " actually happens so in the world," and since an earthly father would so act, so does the Heavenly Father. But this is to misconstrue the parable, as Nygren has pointed out. On Jülicher's view, he argues, the parable is not " self-evident," and as a proof from human life it is quite unconvincing. An opponent, on appeal being made to human life, could easily have described *another* father who on the return of his prodigal son, knowing the value of a wastrel's fine professions, ordered him first to make good his position by honest work. The son did so, and his probation ended, thanked his father " for the strictness that led to his amendment." Now, the opponent might well claim that " it actually happens so in life," and conclude that " the Heavenly Father acts likewise." No; Jesus did not deduce God's love from men's love. The love of the Father in this parable is not the love of an ordinary human father. It is a sheer grace for the undeserving that Jesus depicts. It is the God who freely forgives the man who has no claim on his forgiveness. It is the God who justifies the ungodly.[6]

If we ask next what the parable teaches about man's salvation, the answer is, Not by works but by a heartfelt confession of his own unworthiness and a casting of himself on God's mercy is man saved. For it is not the " correct " son conscious of no shortcomings — " Lo, all these years have I been slaving for you and I never transgressed your commandment " — but the prodigal son who owns his own sinfulness and throws himself unreservedly on his father's forgiveness — " Father, I have sinned . . . I am no more worthy . . . make me as one of thy hired servants " — that is forgiven, and alone truly knows what the father's love is. As Sanday and Headlam say, " Reduced to its simplest elements justification is simply free forgiveness. The Parable of the Prodigal Son is a picture of it. It expresses the attitude of mind required in the sinner and of the reception

accorded to him by God. At bottom . . . the teaching
of the Gospels is not really different from the teaching of
St. Paul. Only one is tenderly and pathetically human,
where the other is a system of Jewish scholasticism." [7]

This great parable does not stand alone in Jesus' teaching. Beside it we can set that of the Pharisee and the
Publican (Luke xviii. 9–14). Not the Pharisee who pa-
rades his own religious achievements before God, who
" boasts " (as Paul would say) of his " works," but the
Publican who cries out of the sense of his own great unworthiness, " God be merciful to me a sinner," is " justified " (Paul's word) in God's sight. For Jesus comes to
call the sick (Mark ii. 17) and wins for himself the noble
nickname of " friend of publicans and sinners " (Mark ii.
16; Luke vii. 34 = Matt. xi. 19).

Again (to pursue the parallel between Jesus and Paul
still further) the Beatitudes of Matt. v. 3 ff. on " the poor in
spirit," " the mourners," " the meek," the men who " hun-
ger and thirst after righteousness " (i.e. God's salvation; [8]
not primarily moral goodness) find a true spiritual echo in
Paul's words in 1 Cor. i. 18–31, and especially verses 26 ff.:
" For behold your calling (i.e. the fact that you are called),
brethren, how that not many wise after the flesh, not many
mighty, not many noble, are called: but God chose the fool-
ish things of the world, that he might put to shame them
that are wise; and God chose the weak things of the world,
that he might put to shame the things that are strong; and
the base things of the world, and the things that are de-
spised, did God choose, yea and the things that are not,
that he might bring to nought the things that are: that no
flesh should glory before God."

And what is Paul's indictment (in Rom. ii.) of the Jew
who, " glorying in the Law, by his transgression of it dis-
honours God," but a parallel to Jesus' arraignment (in

Matt. xxiii.) of the Scribes and Pharisees as hypocrites,[9] who " cleanse the outside of the cup and of the platter but within are full of extortion and excess," who " outwardly appear righteous but inwardly are full of hypocrisy and iniquity " ?

In short, if Jesus did not explicitly say, as Paul did, that all men are sinners, his words do in fact reveal the situation of men as sinners before God just as certainly as do the theological arguments of St. Paul.

(III) THE SERMON ON THE MOUNT AND THE EPISTLE TO THE ROMANS

But there is yet one more argument to be thrown into the scale of proof. Paradoxical though it sound — at any rate in Liberal ears — it is true to say that " the Sermon on the Mount and the Epistle to the Romans belong together." This is a hard saying — if we study words only. Paul has much to say in Romans about sin (sin as a personified force — with a capital S), Jesus, if we only count specific words for sin, little or nothing in the great Sermon. But to infer that Jesus' view of man's spiritual condition before God is radically different from Paul's, that Jesus by comparison with Paul is less seriously concerned about the gravity of sin — this would be a serious error. In any attempt to appraise our Lord's attitude to sin we can begin by cataloguing actual sins and dispositions which he condemned, as: hypocrisy, ingratitude, lack of compassion, unwillingness to forgive, etc. Then we can proceed to pick out sentences like: " If ye then being evil . . ." (Matt. vii. 11; Q) (how calmly Jesus assumes " the corruption of man's heart ") ; or passages like that about defilement (Mark vii. 14–20) which begins, " the things which proceed out of the man are those that defile the man," and ends " for from within, out of the heart of men evil thoughts proceed, fornications, thefts, murders, adulteries, covetings, wickednesses, deceit, lasciviousness, an evil eye, railing, pride, foolishness: all these evil things proceed from within, and defile the man"; or incidental utterances like "no one is good, no one but God" (Mark x. 19; Moffatt); or terrible words about "offences" (*e.g.,* Matt. xviii. 6–7) — teaching which Paul echoes in Rom. xiv. 13 — all this counts for something, indeed for much, in any study of Jesus' teaching about sin.   Nevertheless we shall never realize how seriously he accounted it till we see that Jesus' view of sin is *an inference from his view of righteousness.*   And that brings us to the Sermon on the Mount.   In the Sermon, and especially in the antitheses of Matt. v. 21–48, Jesus set forth the contrast between the Law interpreted as a code of rules to be carried out as works of righteousness — and God's true will for men.   As of old, Isaiah saw "the Lord sitting upon a throne high and lifted up" and in a blinding flash saw his own sinfulness, even so we may suppose the men on whose ears and hearts first fell the revelation of God's will in the great Sermon, saw the divine ideal and knew how far they came short of it.

From time to time one hears people declare that they "like" the Sermon on the Mount.   It is in fact the most terrible indictment of human nature in all literature. "There is no account of sin to match the Sermon." [10]   Who is sufficient for these merciless moral demands?   Who is able to fulfil them?   Not Tolstoi or any other.   If that is the ideal, God have mercy on us all, sinners.

But let there be no misunderstanding here.   We are not arguing that Jesus made these demands — gave this exposition of God's will for man — merely in order to convince men of their inability to fulfil them.   On the contrary, these demands are *meant* to be fulfilled.   (That is precisely Paul's point in regard to the law: it is meant to be fulfilled.) The question is (and here we appeal to the argument from experience — always a strong one): Are they in fact fulfilled? The answer is that they are not. To Windisch who had criticized this interpretation of Jesus' demands in the great Sermon and argued for their "practicability," Bultmann replies with a question: "Will Windisch then assert that *he* fulfils them? Or does he assume that some other man does? Then why not?"[11]

We are led therefore to conclude from Jesus' teaching that "no one is good" by God's standards, that all men, however virtuous, do "come short of the glory" of God's will as it confronts them in the radical requirements of the Sermon on the Mount. Anger, lustful desire, hatred — all are transgressions of God's will for men. If men succumb to them, as they do, what is left but to acknowledge with St. Paul:

> All have swerved aside,
> All have gone bad,
> There is none who does good, no, not one.
>
> (Rom. iii. 12.)

To sum up. Jesus does not use the same language or thought-forms as the Apostle Paul; he does not speculate about sin's origin, or psychologize about its workings as Paul does. But in their fundamental estimate of man's situation before God, in their essential approach to the problem of sin and salvation, they are indubitably at one.[12]

The way is open for a consideration of our second "proposition of unity" — the New Testament approach to the Atonement.

NOTES

1 See Bultmann, *Glauben und Verstehen,* pp. 188–213, especially pp. 191–202, to which I am deeply indebted.

2 Christ, says Paul (Rom. x. 4), is " the end of the law." The end of the law is Christ because he alone has fulfilled the law (cf. Rom. viii. 3–4).

3 Contrast the parable of the Labourers in the Vineyard with a parallel one in the *Talmud (Strack-Billerbeck,* iv. 292 f.). In the latter a labourer has worked for two hours and yet received a full day's wage. When the others complain about unfairness, the householder replies: " Ah, but this man has *done more in two hours* than you have done during the whole day." It is the same parable but with a different ending — how different! — from Matt. xx. 14 f.

4 We shall return to this point later.

5 See *Strack-Billerbeck,* iv. 1–21.

6 I owe the substance of this paragraph to S. Cave, *The Doctrine of the Work of Christ,* pp. 24 f. An even better illustration of Nygren's point is the story of a certain Prodigal Son who, on turning up in the " far country " of another parish, was advised by the minister there to go home and " his father would kill the fatted calf for him." The Prodigal did so; and, months after, meeting the same minister again, was asked, hopefully: " Well, and did he kill the fatted calf? " " No," was the rueful reply, " but he nearly killed the Prodigal Son! " Who will deny that it sometimes " actually happens so in life "?

7 *Romans,* pp. 36 f. It is no objection to say, as some have said, that this parable contains no reference to the atoning death of Chirst; for (a) Jesus speaks *this* side of the Cross; (b) a parable makes one point: it does not contain a complete theology *in nuce;* (c) the doctrine of the Atonement is based on the whole set of facts presented in the life and teaching of Jesus and in the experience of Christians.

8 To a Greek reader Matt. v. 6 would naturally mean, " Blessed are those who ardently desire to be righteous." But " righteousness " in Hebrew and Aramaic probably meant " vindication," " deliverance," " salvation." See Dodd, *The Bible and the Greeks,* p. 55.

9 When Jesus called the Scribes and Pharisees " hypocrites," he called them not " actors " but " *ungodly* " men. It is true that ὑποκρίτης in Greek means " actor "; but the Aramaic word which Jesus used can hardly have had that meaning: Judaism had no actors and no stage. Furthermore, (1) in the LXX the synonyms for ὑποκρίτης are " ungodly," " lawless," " profane "; and (2) " hypocrisy " in Mark xii. 15 is

" wickedness " in Matt. xxii. 18, just as " hypocrite " in Matt. xxiv. 51 is "unfaithful " in Luke xii. 46. See Hebert, *The Throne of David,* pp. 177 f., who writes: " It is fairly clear then what he was saying. Inwardly, in their secret hearts, these religious men were ungodly men, who had no true reverence for God or fear of Him."

10 Ryder Smith, *The Bible Doctrine of Salvation,* p. 170.

11 *Glauben und Verstehen,* p. 199, note 1.

12 The real difference between Jesus and Paul, which does not directly concern us here, is that for Paul, as for all the first Christians, the New Age has come " with power " in the death, resurrection, and exaltation of Jesus the Messiah. With this great event the period of the law is over; the Spirit has come; the *ecclesia* of God is a reality; righteousness is a *fait accompli;* and Christians are " sons of God " enjoying here and now a foretaste — a first instalment — of the glorious inheritance that God has promised to them that love him.

CHAPTER NINE

THE ATONEMENT

Introduction

"OUR SAVIOUR JESUS CHRIST who gave himself for us that he might redeem us from all iniquity and purify unto himself a people for his own possession." This text from the Epistle to Titus contains all the chief elements in that "story of salvation" which is the burden of the New Testament. "Our Saviour Jesus Christ" was the theme of our first section as "a people for his own possession" was the theme of the second. Of the "iniquity" from which men must be redeemed, if there is to be any true salvation, we said something in the preceding chapter. The words remaining in the text, "who gave himself for us that he might redeem us," are therefore the proper theme of our closing chapter. In other words, we are concerned with the Atonement; our aim is not to expound the distinctive teachings of the various New Testament writers on the Atonement — that these exist we freely admit — but to show that there is among these writers a substantial agreement in their thinking about "the word of the Cross."

Jesus came not so much to preach a doctrine of the Atonement as that there might be an Atonement to preach. "*He is* the means of Atonement," [1] as John says (1 John ii. 2). Yet Jesus has not left us wholly ignorant of how he regarded his death, albeit his words are often highly figurative ("a baptism," "a ransom," "a cup"); and as we study the teaching of the New Testament writers on the Atonement, we shall observe how at this point or that they echo the declared mind of their Lord on his death.

As on previous occasions, let our first word be of diversity. When we think of the doctrine of the Atonement in the New Testament, our first thought (such is the influence of the analytical method) is of the variety of theological treatment which the death of Christ receives at the hands of the several New Testament writers. Thus, when we think of St. Paul, texts like Gal. iii. 13 or 2 Cor. v. 21 inevitably suggest a theory of " penal substitution." When we think of the First Epistle of St. Peter, we remember such a passage as " Christ also suffered for you, leaving you *an example* that you should follow his steps " (ii. 21) and we tend to associate Peter with some sort of " exemplarist " view, wherein the Cross is a divine object-lesson in self-sacrifice. We no sooner think of Hebrews than there rises in our mind the sublime representation of Jesus as the one great Sacrifice, and we put the author down as the first expositor of the " sacrificial " view. And when we think of " John," or at any rate the Gospel that he wrote, we decide — after some searching for a brief descriptive label — that perhaps his might be named a " redemption-through-revelation " view; his main argument being that God decisively reveals himself in Christ, especially in his death, and by thus revealing himself redeems men.

So we are wont to think, consciously or unconsciously; and we have some warrant for so doing. For each writer has his own point of view; his own coign of vantage from which he surveys the Cross; his own emphasis for that particular aspect of the " manifold wisdom of God " in the death of Christ which has found and gripped him. Nevertheless deeper than all their differences we can trace a unity of approach among these apostolic men to that Death which was to all " the hiding-place of God's power and the inspiration of all Christian praise."

Indeed, we have St. Paul's authority for believing that there was such a unity of approach. In 1 Cor. xv. 3 Paul reminds his readers that he had " delivered " to them a piece of Christian " tradition " the first part of which declared, " that Christ died for our sins according to the scriptures." (That " tradition " must go back to within a decade of the Crucifixion.[2]) After some further quotation Paul sums up: " Whether therefore it be I or they (that is, I Paul, or they, Peter, James, John, etc.), this is how (the effect to which) we preach and this is how you believed " (1 Cor. xv. 11). The natural inference is surely this: there was no Gospel known in the Primitive Church which had not this as its foundation — that " Christ died for our sins according to the Scriptures." To be sure, it is a very simple statement; but simple as it is, it contains three propositions about the Atonement:

(1) Christ's death was vicarious: ($\upsilon\pi\epsilon\rho$ = on behalf of).
(2) It was related to human sin.
(3) It fulfilled certain scriptures. (These are not specified; but if the reference is not general, Isaiah liii. must surely be intended.)

When we remember the common allegation that Paul was the inventor of the Church's belief in the atoning death of Jesus, it is very reassuring to have from St. Paul's own pen not only a denial of that allegation but an explicit statement that all the earliest preachers held that Christ's death was vicarious, had to do with sin, and fulfilled the Scriptures. Our study of what the apostolic writers have to say about the death of Christ will confirm and amplify this claim.

" God commendeth his own love toward us," wrote

St. Paul, " in that while we were yet sinners Christ died for us " (Rom. v. 8). That noble sentence needs only some such supplement as " in order to reconcile us to himself," to be a fine summary of what the New Testament has to say about the Atonement. It originates in the gracious will of God; it is necessitated by men's sin; its means is Christ, and especially Christ crucified, and its purpose is reconciliation, or restored fellowship, with God. In considering the New Testament teaching on the Atonement we shall therefore treat it as it concerns first, God; then sin; then Christ in his saving work for men; and finally, reconciliation or restored fellowship.

(i) God and the Atonement

Our first thesis is that all our main New Testament writers affirm that Christ's death originated in the (gracious) purpose of God.

Jesus himself had so regarded his Passion. We need only now recall his words at Cæsarea Philippi and in Gethsemane. " The Son of Man," he says, " *must* (δεῖ) suffer many things . . ." (Mark viii. 31). He does not say " it is probable," or " it is humanly certain." He says " it *must* be." It is " the δεῖ of divine necessity." God's will points that way and must be fulfilled. If in the Garden he prays for the removal of the " cup," his final words show that he regards that cup as given him by God, " Howbeit not what I will but what thou wilt " (Mark xiv. 36).

The Primitive Church, whose *kerygma* is preserved in the early speeches of Acts, believed that Christ's death was divinely willed: " Him, being delivered up by the *determinate counsel* and foreknowledge of God, ye by the hand of lawless men did crucify and slay " (Acts ii. 23). The same thought recurs in Acts iv. 27 f.; where Peter declares that the crucifiers have made themselves the instruments of God's purpose for his "holy servant Jesus."

We might muster many passages from his epistles to prove that Paul similarly related Christ's death to the redeeming purpose of God: two will suffice. In the *exordium* of Galatians he writes, "Our Lord Jesus Christ who gave himself for our sins . . . according to the *will* of our God and Father" (Gal. i. 3 f.). In Romans viii. Paul says that God "*sent*" his own Son . . . as an offering for sin " (verse 3), and "*delivered*" him *up* for us all " (verse 32) (cf. Rom. iii. 25, "whom God *set forth* publicly as an expiation," and 1 Thess. v. 9).

First Peter yields no explicit statement that Christ's death was part of " God's Plan "; yet the idea is implied in verses 18–20 of the first chapter. " You were redeemed," says the writer, " with precious blood . . . even the blood of Christ, who was *foreknown* indeed before the foundation of the world."

One passage at least in Hebrews shows that the writer regarded the death of Jesus as lying deep in the Providence of God. It is ii. 9 f., where, after declaring that it was " by God's grace " that Jesus tasted death for every man, the writer declares that the perfecting of " the Pioneer [3] of their salvation " through sufferings was a part of God's great purpose " in bringing many sons to glory " (cf. also iii. 1 f. and v. 1–5 which emphasize the idea of Christ's " appointment " by God to his saving work).

Finally, the idea receives noble expression in the Fourth Gospel and First Epistle of St. John. " As Moses lifted up the serpent in the wilderness," says the Gospel, " even so *must* the Son of Man be lifted up. . . . For God so loved the world, that he *gave* his only begotten Son, that whosoever believeth on him should not perish, but have eternal life " (John iii. 14–16). Of which the counterpart in the Epistle runs: " Herein is love, not that we loved God but that he loved us, and sent his Son to be the expiation for our sins " (1 John iv. 10). The " one-ness of purpose " between God and Jesus in regard to his death is implied in John x. 17 f.

Here, then, is our first evidence of that unity of approach among the New Testament writers to the death of Christ which we are seeking. Not one alone but all our witnesses declare that the Atonement originates in the redeeming purpose of God. And for that word " redeeming " we might almost substitute the word " loving "; for three of our witnesses go that little way farther and attribute the Atonement to the love of God. " God commendeth his love . . . ," says St. Paul (Rom. v. 8); " God so loved the world . . . ," says St. John (John iii. 16); " that by the *grace* of God," says Hebrews (ii. 9), " he might taste death for every man."

(ii) Sin and the Atonement

It is man's sin that creates the problem of the Atonement; for sin sets up a barrier between God and man, and sunders that fellowship with Himself for which God designed man. Therefore it is not surprising that the New Testament writers all define the death of the Saviour in relation to sin.

It is an odd fact that none of Jesus' recorded sayings expressly connect his Passion with sin. But who can doubt that such a connexion did exist in the mind of One who knew himself divinely ordained to fulfil the destiny of the Suffering Servant of Isaiah liii.? Moreover, " when he spoke of giving his life as a ransom for many, he saw the many as sinners, and when he described his blood as covenant-blood, he was thinking of their reconciliation, in spite of sin, to God." [4]

That the Primitive Church made this connexion, our study of 1 Cor. xv. 3 ("Christ died for our sins") has already shown. The Apostolic *kerygma* in Acts contains no such unequivocal statement; but the twin facts that in it Jesus appears as "The Servant" and that forgiveness of sin is offered in his name (Acts ii. 38, v. 31, x. 43), are surely proof that the absence of a clear text on the matter is sheer accident. Indeed, the description of the crucifixion as "hanging on a tree" (Acts v. 30, x. 39; cf. Gal. iii. 13 and 1 Pet. ii. 24) is possibly a hint that Paul was not the first to think of Jesus as enduring in his Passion God's judgment on sin.

When we turn to St. Paul, the connexion between Christ's death and sin is abundantly attested. Not only does Paul share the conviction of his predecessors in this regard (as in 1 Cor. xv. 3), but he elaborates it in his own original way: "God," he says, "set Christ forth publicly as a means of atonement . . . because of the passing over of sins done aforetime" (Rom. iii. 25); or "God sending his own Son . . . as an offering for sin condemned sin in the flesh" (Rom. viii. 3); or (more simply) "our Lord Jesus Christ who gave himself for our sins" (Gal. i. 4).

First Peter yields equally clear evidence: "Who his own self bare our sins in his own body on the tree" (ii. 24; cf. iii. 18).

So does Hebrews. Here the connexion between Christ's death and sin is, we may say, *sacrificially* clear. Christ in his death is the one supreme and final Sacrifice for sins. "When he had by himself purged our sins (i. 3) . . . but now once at the end of the ages hath he been manifested to put away sin by the sacrifice of himself (ix. 26) . . . Christ also having been once offered to bear the sins of many (ix.

28) . . . when he had offered one sacrifice for sins for ever (x. 12) . . ." so running our eye down the column of the concordance we obtain evidence enough and to spare.

Last of all, St. John takes his stand on the same ground. " Behold the Lamb of God," says the Baptist, " that taketh away the sin of the world " (i. 29). Later in the Gospel, as the Passion approaches, Jesus is made to say, " Now is the Judgment of this world: now shall the prince of this world be cast out " (xii. 31). These verses show that the Fourth Evangelist connected the death of Jesus with the removal of sin and the vanquishment of the Devil. In the first Epistle that connexion is much clearer: " The blood of Jesus his Son cleanseth us from all sin " (i. 7); " He is the Expiation for our sins; and not for ours only but also for the whole world " (ii. 2; cf. also iv. 10).

Once again, on this connexion between the death of Christ and sin, our witnesses are unanimous. True, " connexion " is a vague enough word. If we pressed for a fuller explanation of the connexion, we might find that our several witnesses construed the word very differently, one saying perhaps that Christ in his death " revealed " our sin, another that he " bore " our sin, and another that he " expiated " it. But these possible differences are not our immediate business. To the common conviction of the New Testament writers that Christ's death lay deep in the gracious purpose of God we can add a second — that it had to do with human sin.

(iii) Christ and the Atonement

Our third " proposition of unity " concerns the work of Christ for men, and is threefold: all our chief New Testament writers maintain that the saving work of Christ for men consummated by his death is (a) vicarious, i.e. " on

our behalf "; (*b*) representative, *i.e.* " in our name "; and
(*c*) sacrificial, *i.e.* an offering to God fraught with spiritual
virtue for us men.

(a) *Vicarious*

Jesus believed that his death would have vicarious value.
This follows at once from the fact that he knew himself
called to fulfil the destiny of the Suffering Servant; and it
comes to expression in such sayings as " The Son of Man
came not to be served but to serve and to give his life as a
ransom for many " (Mark x. 45), and " This is my blood
of the covenant which is shed *for* (ὑπέρ) many " (Mark
xiv. 24).

Indeed the vicarious nature of Christ's death as it occurs
in the apostolic writers is largely bound up with the preposition ὑπέρ (" on behalf of," " in the interests of ").[5]
That the Primitive Church believed in the vicarious virtue
of Christ's death is proved, first, by that fragment of early
tradition which declared " that Christ died *for* our sins "
(1 Cor. xv. 3); and second, by the *kerygma's* description of
Jesus as " the Servant " of God.

It seems hardly necessary to adduce evidence that Paul
believed in the vicarious value of Christ's death.[6]   Such a
saying as " The Son of God who loved me and gave himself
for me " (Gal. ii. 20) shows how Paul had made his own
the truth which he had " received."   And his pages are
strewn with sentences like: " While we were yet weak,
in due season Christ died *for* the ungodly " (Rom. v. 6);
" He delivered him up *for* us all " (Rom. viii. 32); and
salvation is through our Lord Jesus Christ " who died *for*
us " (1 Thess. v. 9 f.).

First Peter continues the chain of evidence, as three brief
phrases, " for our sake " (i. 20), " *for* you " (ii. 21), and
" our sins " (ii. 24) show.

In Hebrews the vicarious purpose of Christ's death is said to have been " that by the grace of God he might taste death *for* every man " (ii. 9); as its effect is indicated by the question, " How much more shall the blood of Christ, who through the eternal spirit offered *himself* without blemish unto God, cleanse *your* conscience from dead works to serve the living God? " (ix. 14).

St. John, our last witness, is equally emphatic; first, in the word of Christ in the Gospel, " I lay down my life *for* the sheep " (x. 15); then in " the unconscious prophecy " of Caiaphas, " It is expedient for you that one man should die *for* the people " (xi. 50); and, finally, in that noble verse of the Epistle (iii. 16), " Hereby know we love, because he laid down his life *for* us."

(b) *Representative*

(Here in the nature of the case we retread some of the ground covered in the previous section.)

Jesus regarded his death as representative. " The Son of Man " (as we have already argued) is a representative figure. So is the Suffering Servant. Jesus interpreted the one by the other with reference to his death: " The Son of Man came not to be served but to serve and to give his life as a ransom for many " (Mark x. 45). If this does not mean that Jesus the Servant Son of Man in dying represents " the many," it means nothing at all (cf. Mark xiv. 24).

The brief references to Christ's death in the Primitive Church's *kerygma* yields no explicit evidence for the idea of representation. But it is *implicit* in the characterization of Jesus as " the Servant of God."

For Paul, Christ was " the inclusive Representative " of the New Humanity as Adam was of the Old.[7] And Christ fulfilled his representative ministry supremely in his death:

"For as through the *one* man's disobedience the *many* were constituted sinners, even so through the obedience of the *one* shall the *many* be constituted righteous" (Rom. v. 19). The same thought of Christ's representative suffering appears in 2 Cor. v. 14: "The love of Christ (*i.e.* Christ's love for us) constraineth us; because we thus judge that one died *for* [8] all, therefore all died," *i.e.* in Him who is the inclusive representative of all.

The representative aspect of Christ's death emerges in 1 Peter when he writes: "Christ also suffered for sins once, the righteous for the unrighteous" (iii. 18; cf. ii. 24).

More fully than any other New Testament writer does the unknown *Auctor ad Hebræos* emphasize the representative character of Christ's death. For in this epistle Jesus is the great High Priest, and whatever else a high priest may be, he is one who represents men before God. In such a passage as vii. 26 f., the representative aspect of Christ's atoning sacrifice is very clear: "For such a high priest became us, holy, guileless, undefiled, separated from sinners, and made higher than the heavens; who needeth not daily, like those high priests, to offer up sacrifices, first for his own sins, and then for the sins of the people: for this he did once for all, when he offered up himself."

Less fundamental in John's thinking than in that of Hebrews, the idea of Christ's representative death appears in "the unconscious prophecy" of Caiaphas (John xi. 50–52); and in the First Epistle it finds striking expression in the claim that Christ is our "Advocate," or "Intercessor" with the Father and is himself the Expiation for the world's sin (ii. 1 f., iv. 10).

Thus, the New Testament writers are at one in holding not only that Christ "died for sinners," but also that in his dying he "represented" them before God.

(c) *Sacrificial*

All our New Testament writers regard Christ's death as a sacrifice. Paul, Peter, *Auctor ad Hebræos,* John — all see the Death of Christ from one sacrificial angle or another. Of course the emphasis varies a good deal: Hebrews has a vast deal more to say about the Atonement as a Sacrifice than the Fourth Gospel. Moreover, though they all use Old Testament sacrificial language, no particular Old Testament sacrifice is adopted by all the New Testament writers as " an analogue *par excellence"* to the death of Christ. If covenant sacrifice is prominent (cf. Ex. xxiv.), the Passover and the sin-offering are also employed to express the meaning of Christ's death. And besides references to particular Old Testament sacrifices we find our writers freely using words with a sacrificial connotation — " cleansing," " expiation," and the like.

Perhaps a brief summary of the evidence will serve our purpose best at this point.

Jesus himself regarded his death as a sacrifice. Consider the two primary accounts of the Last Supper (1 Cor. xi. 23 ff.; Mark xiv. 22 ff.). Both accounts, though independent, must go back to a common original. Here is the common original as paraphrased by Lietzmann [9] : " I am the sacrificial victim whose blood is poured out for you, that is, for the believing People, to seal a new Covenant with God, and whose body is slain for you." Every one of the words Jesus employs — " blood " (Lev. xvii. 11), " covenant " (Ex. xxiv. 8), " poured out " (Lev. iv. 7, 8, etc.), " body " — has a sacrificial association.

Our scanty evidence concerning the doctrine of the Primitive Church before Paul's time does not enable us to say certainly that Paul's predecessors interpreted Christ's death in sacrificial terms. But when we recall their conviction that " Christ died for our sins," remember that most of them were Jews, and observe that all the later apostolic writers thought of Christ's death as a sacrifice, we may infer that those who were first " in Christ " did so too.

The chief passage in which Paul describes the death of Christ as a sacrifice is Rom. iii. 24 f. with its reference to " expiation " and " blood." To this passage we must add numerous allusions to redemption by the " blood " of Christ (allusions not to his violent death as such, but to this *life sacrificially released by death*); 1 Cor. v. 7, where Christ is called the Passover Lamb; and Eph. v. 2, " Even as Christ also loved you, and gave himself up for us, an *offering* and a *sacrifice* to God for an odour of a sweet smell " (cf. Rom. viii. 3 ($\pi\epsilon\rho\grave{\iota}$ $\tau\hat{\eta}s$ $\dot{a}\mu a\rho\tau\acute{\iota}as$)).

First Peter clearly regards Christ's death as a sacrifice. The opening allusion to " sprinkling of the blood of Jesus Christ " (i. 2) [10]; the following reference to redemption by the blood of Christ, " the lamb without blemish and spot " (i. 18 f.); and, finally, ii. 24, all point the same sacrificial way.

To quote proof texts from Hebrews would mean quoting most of the Epistle. From beginning to end the writer conceives Christ's death in terms of sacrifice. All the vocabulary of sacrifice is used to prove that Christ's death for men in complete obedience to the will of God is the perfect fulfilment of what the Levitical sacrificial system vainly tried to achieve. For the writer, Jesus is

> That only offering perfect in Thine eyes,
> The one true, pure, immortal sacrifice.

If in the Fourth Gospel sacrificial language is not abundant — we think of i. 29 (" the lamb of God "), vi. 53–58 (the eucharistic sayings), and xvii. 19 (" for their sakes I sanctify myself ") — " John " fills up this lack in his homily, where he alludes to the " cleansing " power of Jesus' " blood " (1 John ii. 7), and twice (ii. 2 and iv. 10) declares the " expiatory " virtue of Christ's death.

Thus, not one but all of the chief New Testament writers follow their Lord by interpreting his saving work on their behalf in sacrificial terms. One point more, and that of capital importance, falls to be added. In the Old Testament the sacrificial principle had received its profoundest and most spiritual expression in the figure of the Servant of the Lord whose humiliation and death would have (so the great unknown prophet of the Exile said) sin-atoning power for " the many." In the figure of the Servant, Jesus himself saw his own tragic but glorious destiny prefigured, and used the words of Isaiah liii. to describe the purpose of his dying (Mark x. 45, xiv. 24, etc.). It is a proof at once of their fidelity to the mind of Jesus and of their essential unity of approach to the problem of the Cross that each of the chief New Testament writers, when he comes to speak of it, employs the language of Isaiah liii. Thus, starting with the Primitive Church, we note the description of Jesus as " the Servant " of God (Acts iii. 13, iv. 27, 30; cf. viii. 30–35). Twice Paul borrows the language of Isaiah liii., namely, in Rom. iv. 24 and Phil. ii. 6–11.[11] 1 Pet. ii. 21–25 is shot through with language from the same chapter. The *Auctor ad Hebræos* echoes Isa. liii. 12 in ix. 28; and, as Nairne observes,[12] " the Epistle would be easier to understand if the author had called our Lord's high-priesthood ' priesthood after the order of the Suffering Servant ' instead of ' after the order of Melchizedek.' " Finally, most exegetes find an echo in Isaiah liii. in St. John i. 29 (and 36): " Behold the lamb of God which taketh away the sin of the world " (see, *e.g.* Bernard, St. John, *ad loc.*),

an echo that is even clearer if " lamb " here is a mistrans-
lation of an Aramaic word (*talya'*) which also meant
" servant." [13]

(iv) The Spiritual End of the Atonement

Finally, the New Testament writers show a general
agreement as to the spiritual end or object of God's atoning work in Christ. That spiritual end is a restoration of
the living and loving fellowship between God and man
rendered impossible by man's sin and guilt — in short,
reconciliation.

Though Jesus in the Synoptic Gospels says no explicit
word about it, it is surely implicit in his covenant-saying
at the Last Supper, more especially if Paul's version of the
saying is original. For "this cup is the *new covenant* in
my blood " has as its spiritual background the great prophecy of Jer. xxxi. 31 ff. The supreme blessing of that new
dispensation to which Jeremiah looks forward is a new and
intimate fellowship between God and his People based on
the forgiveness of all their sins:

> For I will forgive their iniquity
> And their sin will I remember no more.

This, then, is the spiritual end which Jesus believed that his
death would achieve, and may we not add that in his story
of the returning Prodigal's welcome by his father he has
given us an immortal picture of it?

We are often told that the earliest preachers were not
conscious theologians. Yet when they promised the forgiveness of sins in Jesus' name to those who by repentance
and faith accepted their *kerygma* of Christ crucified, risen,
and exalted (Acts ii. 38, iii. 19, x. 43) they were not un-
aware that the supreme blessing resulting from God's

mighty act in Christ was a renewed fellowship founded
on the forgiveness of sin.

Paul uses many words to describe the spiritual end
achieved by God's atoning work in Christ: " justification "
(*e.g.* Rom. iii. 24), " peace with God " (Rom. v. 1), " access " (Rom. v. 2), " life " (1 Thess. v. 10); but perhaps
his favourite word is " reconciliation " (Rom. v. 10 f.; 2
Cor. v. 18 f., etc.), that is, a restoration of fellowship between God and man.

Peter puts the matter in one clear and short sentence:
" Christ also suffered for our sins once . . . that he might
conduct us to God " (1 Pet. iii. 18).

The theme of Hebrews is nothing more or less than
" *access* " to God through Jesus the perfect High Priest and
Sacrifice: " Having therefore, brethren, boldness to enter
into the Holy Place by the blood of Jesus by . . . a new
and living way through the veil . . . let us *draw near* "
(Heb. x. 19 ff.).

For John the supreme blessing offered to men in Christ
is comprehensively described as " eternal life "; and this
" life " is the fruit of Christ's death (John iii. 14 f.). " Eternal life " is in its essence fellowship with God in Christ
(cf. John xvii. 3). A famous text in the Fourth Gospel
gives us St. John's view of the matter: " For their sakes I
sanctify myself that they themselves also may be sanctified
in truth " (John xvii. 19). The reference is to his death,
and the sentence means " that now in his own Person
through death he is about to establish between God and
man a relation which men could never have established for
themselves, but into which they can truly enter." [14] What
is that relation if it be not what John calls in his epistle
" fellowship "; " our fellowship is with the Father and
with his Son Jesus Christ " (1 John i. 3).

To sum up. The Atonement originates in the gracious

will of God; it has to do with sin; its means is the crucified Christ whose death is vicarious, representative, and sacrificial; and the spiritual end which it secures is reconciliation or renewed fellowship with God based on the forgiveness of sins. On these aspects of the Atonement there is general agreement among the various writers of the New Testament. To say that there is one single uniform doctrine of the Atonement in the New Testament would be untrue; to say that there is an essential unity of approach to the problem of the Cross among the writers of the New Testament is the only conclusion possible in the light of the evidence adduced.

One final question remains: how shall we best characterize that " common " view of the Atonement which we have discovered in the New Testament as a whole? Which is the best inclusive category for describing it? The present writer has no doubt that Vincent Taylor is right in choosing the word " sacrifice " for this purpose.

The *aim* of all sacrifice is restored fellowship with God (in the higher forms of religion, fellowship disrupted by sin). Its *medium* is a representative offering — an offering with which the worshippers can identify themselves in their approach to God. Its *rationale* is the offering of life. And its *culminating point* is the sharing in that life by means of a common meal.

If this be a true summary of the general theory of sacrifice, we cannot help observing how similar to it is the " common " view of the Atonement in the New Testament.

First, the aim. If the aim of sacrifice is restored fellowship with God, a fellowship disrupted by man's sin, that, as we have just seen, is precisely the spiritual end which the New Testament writers regard as secured by the Atonement.

Second, the medium: " a representative offering with

which the worshippers can identify themselves in their approach to God." And is not that how the New Testament writers in general and the *Auctor ad Hebræos* in particular regard the work of Christ, which " is vicarious because it is representative, and representative because it is sacrificial," a work with which Christians identify themselves by penitence and faith.

Third, the rationale: " the offering of life ": this is what the New Testament writers mean by the " blood of Christ," life surrendered to God in death and released for men's spiritual appropriation. Of course the idea is ethicized and spiritualized. If we ask *what* Christ offered when he surrendered his life to God the answer will include these two things at the very least:

(*a*) He offered a life of perfect submission to his Father's will, a perfect obedience to God's redemptive purpose.

(*b*) He offered a perfect submission to God's judgment on sin, came under sin's blight, tasted in his life and especially in his death the reaction of God's holy love to the horror of sin.

Fourth, the culminating point: " a sharing in that life by means of a common meal." So Jesus at the Last Supper bade his disciples eat and drink (*i.e.* appropriate the spiritual blessings of) the bread and wine which symbolized his sacrifice of himself. And clearly for St. Paul (1 Cor. x. 14–22) and St. John (vi. 53 ff.) this is a primary purpose of the Eucharist: it is a means of sharing in the spiritual virtue of the atoning death of Christ.

We cannot carry this discussion further now. It must be pursued elsewhere.[15] The description of the Atonement as a sacrifice raises many problems: for example, the problem of the relation of the atoning sacrifice of Christ in time to the eternal sacrifice of God, *i.e.* the problem of understanding the Cross as " the temporal actuality of an eternal reality." [16]   For our purpose we have said enough: we have demonstrated the essential unity of New Testament teaching on the Atonement: we have shown reason for believing that " through the New Testament there runs one mighty thought: Christ died for our sins: he bore what we should have borne: he did for us what we could never have done for ourselves: he did for God that which was God's good pleasure." [17]

As we close this third and last part of our synthetic approach to the theology of the New Testament, two practical observations seem relevant.

First, any presentation of Christianity to-day which claims to be in line with the New Testament must recognize the serious character of the problem of sin.   According to the Bible, sin is not a sign of man's immaturity — " humanity's growing pains " — or of his ignorance, *i.e.* something which education may be expected to cure; it is rebellion against a holy God and involves guilt which must be removed if there is to be any true fellowship between God and man.   The Christian preacher and teacher must set before men the reality of sin, must insist that any view of life that does not face up to the fact of sin is not worth two straws. " The mystery of iniquity " may still remain a mystery; he may still be unable fully to explain how moral evil found entrance into a world made by a good God; but of the reality of sin and its gravity he himself must be in no doubt.   The tragic happenings of our times — the radical perversion of human affairs to-day — are the best evidence to which he can point by way of proof.   Let him wrestle seriously with St. Anselm's words, *Nondum considerasti quanti ponderis sit peccatum,* let him test the truth of the Bible view of sin by a consideration of contemporary events, and then let him by showing man's sinful situation before God reveal his great need of redemption.

Second, hand in hand with this emphasis on the reality of sin must go a renewed preaching of the divine " remedy " for it.

In other words, he must expound the Atonement. It is true that men are saved by the *fact* of the Atonement and not by any theory of it. It is true again that there is no theory of the Atonement taught in the creeds of the Church which can be called orthodox. It is true once again that no theory of the Atonement can claim to be a wholly complete and convincing rationale of what God does for men in the crucified Christ. There will always be a shadow about the Cross —

> But none of the ransomed ever knew
> How deep were the waters crossed.

Nevertheless, if a man is to preach the Cross effectively he must have some theory of it. But there is preaching and preaching of the Cross. There is a preaching of it widely current to-day which sees in the Cross only a revelation of God's love, albeit the supreme one. Better the Cross preached thus than not at all! And it is indeed true, as Paul and John saw and said, that the Cross originates in the loving purpose of God. But for the writers of the New Testament the Cross is immeasurably more than a revelation of God's love; and " unless such a theory can be extended and brought into fuller accord with New Testament teaching, it is no more than an Ark of Refuge from which the theologian looks wistfully for a green leaf of hope in a world of cataclysm. It is the prolegomena to the doctrine of the Atonement, not the doctrine itself." [18] Again, there is a preaching of the Cross which makes Christ on the Tree a divine object-lesson in self-sacrifice. This view of the Cross, though it can find texts for its justification in the New Testament, is no less inadequate. Not because the Cross meant this for them did the New Testament writers find in it "the hiding-place of God's power and the inspiration of all Christian praise." All such preaching of the Cross is peripheral: it never goes to the living centre of things. What we need is a preaching of it with the apostolic emphasis. We must try, using language and forms of thought intelligible to the men of our day, to present the Cross as the New Testament writers present it. And if so, why not in terms of sacrifice as they did? True, the ideas that cluster about sacrifice do not readily come home to modern men. That only shows how urgent is the task of explaining such phrases as "the blood of Christ" in forms that they can understand. But surely the basic idea of sacrifice — an offering which in humble faith the worshipper can make his own — is not intrinsically difficult. And if that is so, it is surely not impossible to make ancillary terms and ideas intelligible too.

There is one final remark to be made. Though the Atonement in the New Testament is presented as a "finished work," it is not something done outside man. Man has to make its benefits his own. The Atonement is not complete until man makes his response to that "love so amazing, so divine" manifested in the Cross. That he does in three ways: first, by faith, when with his sense of sin upon him he puts himself into the hands of the crucified and living Christ for God and eternity; second, in the holy Communion, when — still by faith — he appropriates the spiritual benefits of Christ's Passion symbolized in the broken bread and outpoured wine; and third, by sacrificial living when, remembering what Christ has done for him, he gives himself for others in service and selfless love as He gave himself for us.

NOTES

1 Or "Expiation" (ἱλασμός). See Dodd, *The Bible and the Greeks*, pp. 82–95.

2 Paul probably received it at Damascus when he became a Christian.

3 ἀρχηγός "leader," "pioneer." The "pioneer is the strong swimmer who carries the rope ashore and so not only secures his own position but makes rescue for all who will follow" (Dods, *E.G.T. ad loc.*).

4 V. Taylor, *The Atonement in N.T. Teaching*, p. 89. Matthew's addition of "unto remission of sins" (Matt. xxvi. 28) to Mark's version of the Covenant-saying is generally allowed to be a paraphrase which brings out the true meaning.

5 In what follows we italicize "for" where it represents ὑπέρ.

6 He never uses the preposition ἀντί, "instead of."

7 See Dodd, *Romans*, p. 80.

8 ὑπέρ, not ἀντί: "for the sake of," not "instead of."

9 *Messe und Herrenmahl*, p. 221.

10 Cf. Ex. xxiv. 8.

11 For a discussion of these two passages, see *Paul and his Predecessors*, pp. 33 f. and 45 ff.

12 *Hebrews* (C.G.T.), p. xciv.

13 See Burney, *The Aramaic Origin of the Fourth Gospel*, pp. 107 f. Jeremias in *Kittel's Theol. Voc. sub.* ἀμνός accepts Burney's view: "probably . . . originally in John i. 29, 36 the reference was to Jesus as the Servant of God."

14 Denney, *The Death of Christ*, p. 269.

15 In V. Taylor's books.

16 See H. W. Robinson, *Redemption and Revelation*.

17 J. K. Mozley, *The Doctrine of the Atonement*, p. 93.

18 V. Taylor, *The Atonement in N.T. Teaching*, p. 299.

CHAPTER TEN

SUMMARY AND POSTSCRIPT

B Y WAY OF postscript let us briefly look back on the way that we have travelled.

We began by noting the "centripetal" tendency discernible in recent study of the New Testament and hailing it as a welcome change of direction. The aim which we proposed was a quest for the unity of the New Testament, and the word which best summarized that unity we took to be *Heilsgeschichte*. Such a term held together both Testaments (*i.e.* saw the theme of the New Testament as the consummation of God's saving purpose for his People declared in the Old Testament). It comprised three chief elements: a message of salvation centring in a Saviour; a saved People; and the means of salvation. (Chapter I.)

Then we turned aside for a moment to expose the defects of the analytic approach to the New Testament and to insist on the need for a synthetic approach. Recent research (we said) was making ever plainer the unity of the New Testament, and an appended note showed the equivalence of certain New Testament conceptions apparently unrelated. (Chapter II.)

After defining our critical positions we proceeded to an exposition of our triune theme. (Chapter III.)

(1) One message of salvation, the *kerygma*, runs through the whole New Testament. We recover this *kerygma* from the early speeches in Acts and certain pre-Pauline passages in St. Paul's Epistles. The four Gospels themselves are, in greater or less degree, simply expansions of the

kerygma; and the First Epistle of St. Peter and Hebrews reveal quite unmistakably its influence. In a practical comment we discussed the relevance of the Apostolic *kerygma* for present-day Christian preaching. (Chapter IV.)

The *kerygma* implied a Christology, which might be briefly summed up in the New Testament phrase, " Jesus is Lord." This essential Christology, we showed, pervaded the whole New Testament: the Primitive Church, Paul, Peter, the Synoptists, and John: one and all, while holding fast the humanity of Jesus, set him on the divine side of reality. From this we drew certain practical conclusions for the Christian attitude to Christ to-day. (Chapter V.)

(2) From Christology we passed to Ecclesiology.

Recent research has shown quite conclusively that Jesus set himself the high task of creating a new people of God. Four main arguments were advanced:

(i) The redemptive Rule of God preached and embodied by Jesus implied a people of God living under that Rule.

(ii) Jesus' conception of his Messiahship implied the creation of a new Community.

(iii) The Messianic Shepherd must needs have a Flock.

(iv) In the call, training, and mission of the Twelve we see the nucleus of the new people of God being formed. At the Last Supper Jesus instituted a new Covenant with them. (Chapter VI.)

The next chapter dealt with the " little flock " of Jesus now become as a result of the Resurrection and Pentecost the Apostolic Church. These earliest Christians held four basic convictions about themselves:

(i) They were the *ecclesia* — the true people of God.

(ii) They were united in a common allegiance to Jesus as Lord.

   (iii) They were " the Community of the Spirit."
   (iv) They had a saving mission to fulfil.

These four convictions are integral to all later apostolic thought about the Church, whether it be the writings of Paul, Peter, the writer to the Hebrews, or John. (Chapter VII.)

(3) From Ecclesiology we passed to Soteriology.

Our first contention was that in their essential view of man's sinful situation before God, our Lord and St. Paul were at one. This was shown by a detailed comparison of the teachings of Jesus and of Paul on (*a*) the Law, (*b*) Justification, (*c*) sin as it is exhibited in the Sermon on the Mount and the Epistle to the Romans.

The conclusion was that Jesus no less than Paul held that " all have sinned " and need salvation. (Chapter VIII.)

Finally, we sought to show that in their approach to the Atonement the New Testament writers show substantial agreement. Thus, all our New Testament witnesses agree that:

   (i) The Atonement originates in the redeeming Will of God.
   (ii) It has to do with man's sin.
   (iii) Christ's saving work is (*a*) vicarious, (*b*) representative, (*c*) sacrificial.
   (iv) The spiritual end secured by the Atonement is restored fellowship between God and man.

With this " common " New Testament view of the Atonement before us we ventured to offer some closing observations on the proper preaching of the Atonement to-day. (Chapter IX.)

There is, therefore, a deep unity in the New Testament,

which dominates and transcends all the diversities. We have tried to show the lines along which the unity is to be found. No claim is made that all the evidence has been collected. What we do claim is that the approach is the right one, and we must hope that all future text-books on New Testament theology will be written from this synthetic point of view. Of the analytic text-books with their series of " separate-compartment " chapters, each bearing its label — Synoptic, Pauline, Johannine, etc. — we have already more than enough.

It would be idle to pretend that all our scholars see the unity of the New Testament or feel the need for the sort of text-books which we desiderate. A distinguished Liberal scholar on hearing of the writer's intention to write this book replied that " the unity of the New Testament had never been in dispute." And it chanced that as this postscript was being written the writer lighted on a little book entitled *The New Testament To-day,* by that well-known New Testament scholar, Professor E. F. Scott, in which occurs the following sentence: " Every teacher (*i.e.* of the Primitive Church) seems to have had his own interpretation of what was meant by the Gospel, and the New Testament, so far from reflecting an original agreement, is the record of this diversity of Christian thought." [1] We have no desire to deny the diversities; indeed, from time to time we have chosen to indicate them; but in the light of the evidence adduced in this book we submit that such a judgment on the New Testament is quite one-sided and wholly misleading. No wonder books written from such a point of view arouse in the average reader's mind the perplexed question: " If each writer has his own view of the Gospel, which is the right one? "

It is for men so perplexed that we have written. This book tries, however inadequately, to tell the ordinary thoughtful Christian what the central message of the New Testament is; it finds in the New Testament the record of the completion of God's saving purpose for his People through the sending of his Son the Messiah; it seeks to show that for all the New Testament writers there is one Lord, one Church, one Salvation.

These are great days for theology. The Queen of the Sciences is once again coming into her own. Men are beginning to see that a Christianity without a theology is not Christianity at all; and they are turning back, some to Luther or Calvin, some to Thomas Aquinas. Some of us, with no disrespect for these great names, feel that the theology which the age needs should be built primarily on New Testament foundations. But, whatever be our views, all are realizing anew the importance of Biblical theology, and the paramount importance of the New Testament. So we send forth this little book in the hope that it may meet the need of many who, dissatisfied and even mystified by the older text-books on the theology of the New Testament, are yet convinced that through it runs one message, that from its beginning to its end there is a grand agreement concerning that " so great salvation " of which every one of its writers speaks and concerning that Person whose is " the only name under heaven whereby we must be saved."

NOTE

1 P. 40.